THE BEDFORD SERIES IN HISTORY AND CULTURE

Nathan the Wise

by Gotthold Ephraim Lessing

WITH RELATED DOCUMENTS

Related Titles in
THE BEDFORD SERIES IN HISTORY AND CULTURE
Advisory Editors: Natalie Zemon Davis, *Princeton University*
Ernest R. May, *Harvard University*
Lynn Hunt, *University of California, Los Angeles*
David W. Blight, *Yale University*

THE BEDFORD SERIES IN HISTORY AND CULTURE

Nathan the Wise
by Gotthold Ephraim Lessing
WITH RELATED DOCUMENTS

Translated, Edited, and with an Introduction by

Ronald Schechter
College of William and Mary

BEDFORD/ST. MARTIN'S   Boston   ♦   New York

For Bedford/St. Martin's

Publisher for History: Patricia A. Rossi
Director of Development for History: Jane Knetzger
Developmental Editor: Michael Weber
Associate Editor, Publishing Services: Maria Teresa Burwell
Senior Marketing Manager: Jenna Bookin Barry
Project Management: Books By Design, Inc.
Text Design: Claire Seng-Niemoeller
Indexing: Books By Design, Inc.
Cover Design: Billy Boardman
Cover Illustration: The final scene of *Nathan the Wise* from *Gotthold Ephraim Lessings
  sämtliche Schriften. Achtzehnter Theil.* [The Complete Writings of Gotthold Ephraim
  Lessing. Eighteenth Part.] (Berlin, 1793). Copper engraving by Casper Weinrauch.
  By permission of the Herzog August Bibliothek Wolfenbüttel.
Composition: Stratford Publishing Services
Printing and Binding: Haddon Craftsmen, an RR Donnelley & Sons Company

President: Joan E. Feinberg
Editorial Director: Denise Wydra
Director of Marketing: Karen Melton Soeltz
Director of Editing, Design, and Production: Marcia Cohen
Manager, Publishing Services: Emily Berleth

Library of Congress Control Number: 2003108785

Copyright © 2004 by Bedford/St. Martin's

Manufactured in the United States of America.

9 8 7 6 5 4
f e d c b a

For information, write: Bedford/St. Martin's, 75 Arlington Street, Boston, MA 02116
(617-399-4000)

ISBN: 0-312-44243-2
EAN: 978-0-312-44243-9

Foreword

The Bedford Series in History and Culture is designed so that readers can study the past as historians do.

The historian's first task is finding the evidence. Documents, letters, memoirs, interviews, pictures, movies, novels, or poems can provide facts and clues. Then the historian questions and compares the sources. There is more to do than in a courtroom, for hearsay evidence is welcome, and the historian is usually looking for answers beyond act and motive. Different views of an event may be as important as a single verdict. How a story is told may yield as much information as what it says.

Along the way the historian seeks help from other historians and perhaps from specialists in other disciplines. Finally, it is time to write, to decide on an interpretation and how to arrange the evidence for readers.

Each book in this series contains an important historical document or group of documents, each document a witness from the past and open to interpretation in different ways. The documents are combined with some element of historical narrative—an introduction or a biographical essay, for example—that provides students with an analysis of the primary source material and important background information about the world in which it was produced.

Each book in the series focuses on a specific topic within a specific historical period. Each provides a basis for lively thought and discussion about several aspects of the topic and the historian's role. Each is short enough (and inexpensive enough) to be a reasonable one-week assignment in a college course. Whether as classroom or personal reading, each book in the series provides firsthand experience of the challenge—and fun—of discovering, recreating, and interpreting the past.

Natalie Zemon Davis
Ernest R. May
Lynn Hunt
David W. Blight

Preface

Nathan the Wise by Gotthold Ephraim Lessing is one of the great works of the Age of Enlightenment. Repudiating a world view governed by prejudice and blind adherence to dogma, it affirms the essential humanity of people whom Christendom had long portrayed as inferior. Jews, Muslims, and Christians, according to Lessing, all equally deserve respect and have equal claims on religious truth. This message of human equality is arguably the eighteenth century's single most important contribution to Western civilization and, of course, a major reason why the Enlightenment is studied in Western civilization classes.

The fact that in *Nathan* this message was propagated by a German writer, Lessing, in Germany, a country that still conjures images of totalitarianism and genocide in the minds of many, is worth emphasizing.

Western civilization textbooks and instructors nearly always teach the importance of the French Enlightenment, but they often overlook the German Enlightenment. This edition of *Nathan the Wise,* which includes a substantive introduction and relevant supplementary documents in addition to the complete text of Lessing's play, can help remedy that omission. Similarly, this volume may serve as a useful text for courses that focus on the Enlightenment itself, as instructors of such courses often lack accessible translations of important German authors. It can also enrich classes in German and in Jewish history, since Lessing's play will powerfully remind readers that German anti-Semitism was neither natural nor inevitable.

Nor is *Nathan* conducive to an understanding only of the past. Its theme of reconciliation among the three great monotheistic religions—Judaism, Christianity, and Islam—is of the most urgent relevance today. I began this project before September 11, 2001, and was then thinking principally of the prolonged conflict in Israel and Palestine. It seemed to me that Lessing's classic story of religious harmony in Jerusalem at the time of the Crusades provided such a vivid contrast to the news of endless contemporary violence in the Middle East that it should be made available to students who might otherwise see the situation there as hopeless. On September 11, the strife "there" suddenly came "here"; although the conflict in the Middle East was never simply a local one, its global ramifications became quickly and painfully clear. Since that day, suspicion, antipathy, and conflict among adherents of these three religions—and those who claim to be acting on their behalf—have only escalated. Obviously it would be naïve to expect a book to cure the world of such poisonous feelings, but envisioning the common humanity of Jews, Christians, and Muslims is surely a necessary condition for any future reconciliation. *Nathan* not only provides such a vision but also affirms different perspectives, religious and otherwise, as a positive feature of humanity.

FEATURES OF THIS EDITION

I have prepared this edition of *Nathan the Wise* expressly for today's college students. The complete play has been newly translated by me. (I discuss how I went about translating the work in the note on the text and translation that follows this preface.) Where needed, I have added glosses to the text of the play as footnotes that explain historical references, literary allusions, and the like. Currently there is one other English translation of *Nathan* in print, but it is neither addressed to nor translated for today's students and—perhaps most unfortunate of all—leaves out six entire scenes.

A general introduction to this text provides appropriate background and context for students. I first briefly discuss Lessing's career and how he challenged the conventions of his time. Then I explore the condition of the Jews in eighteenth-century Europe: the prejudice and discrimination they suffered, the Enlightenment and Jewish emancipation, and the significance of the life and work of Lessing's friend, the Jewish philosopher Moses Mendelssohn. Following a summary of the plot of *Nathan the Wise,* I consider how the play illustrates Lessing's approach to religious diversity and the problem of intolerance. Finally, I discuss the play's contemporary reception and its relevance for today.

To supplement Lessing's work and to help place it in historical context, this edition includes five eighteenth-century documents that I have excerpted and translated. The first, Johann Andrea Eisenmenger's *Jewry*

Revealed (Frankfurt, 1700; Berlin, 1711), is a compilation of anti-Semitic accusations, including ritual murder, that were still current when Lessing was writing. Eisenmenger's infamous screed is followed by a proposal by the Prussian reformer Christian Wilhelm von Dohm, *On the Civic Improvement of the Jews* (Berlin, 1781). This reading combats Eisenmenger's libels, and though Dohm is not entirely free of prejudice, he insists that the Jews' shortcomings are no different from those of any people placed in disadvantageous circumstances and that discriminatory laws against them should be lifted. Although it is unclear whether Dohm read *Nathan,* his book, appearing just two years after Lessing's play, reflects the Enlightenment currents that made it possible for writers to question anti-Semitic prejudices and their consequences in law and society. The third document is an excerpt from François-Louis-Claude Marin's *History of Saladin* (Paris, 1758). It provides a contemporary European perspective on Muslims in general and especially on the historical figure Saladin, who plays a central role in *Nathan.* Moreover, since Lessing is known to have read this book, the excerpt sheds light on the process by which the playwright researched his subject. The fourth document is from the writings of Moses Mendelssohn, the Jewish philosopher who served as the model for the character of Nathan. Mendelssohn understood Lessing's play as an affirmation of God's power and of the ultimate goodness of God's plan for humanity. This reading, which explains why *Nathan* was an "anti-Candide," places the play in the context of eighteenth-century debates about optimism, or the belief that "everything is for the best." The last document, excerpted from Gottfried Wilhelm Leibniz's *Theodicy* (Berlin, 1710), presents the fundamental articulation of that belief and contains a lucid summary of its arguments. The Leibniz reading provides the essential philosophical background for Lessing's thinking.

This volume includes several additional teaching tools. Each document is introduced with a headnote that supplies essential historical context. Questions for students to consider appear near the end of the volume. Both headnotes and questions are intended to aid students in focusing on what is important in the texts; the questions can also serve to stimulate discussion in class and as topics for writing assignments. Immediately following the text of the play is a chronology of Lessing's life. The volume concludes with a selected bibliography of books and articles on Lessing, *Nathan,* and the German Enlightenment, and an index. Also included in this edition are several relevant illustrations.

ACKNOWLEDGMENTS

Daniel Gordon of the University of Massachusetts, Amherst, has been a role model to me in many ways, and his translation for the Bedford Series in History and Culture edition of Voltaire's *Candide* in particular, with its masterful introduction, provided a model of how to make a historical source and work of literature meaningful to students. He also read an early draft of my *Nathan* edition and offered very helpful criticisms. My friends and colleagues Liliane Weissberg of the University of Pennsylvania and Jonathan Hess of the University of North Carolina at Chapel Hill, who also read this manuscript, have generously lent their expertise as scholars of German literature and culture. Lynn Hunt of the University of California, Los Angeles, provided invaluable advice on making the introduction accessible to students in Western civilization courses. Marion Deshmukh of George Mason University, Lois Dubin of Smith College, and Sophia Rosenfeld of the University of Virginia contributed sage advice as well. Patricia Rossi at Bedford/St. Martin's encouraged this project and shepherded it through the initial stages, and Michael Weber has done his job well by synthesizing various suggestions for revising *Nathan* and gently reminding me not to exceed my deadlines too egregiously. Ute Schechter saved me from embarrassing translation errors, and our son Arthur provided his usual moral support.

Ronald Schechter

A Note about the Text and Translation

For my translation of *Nathan the Wise,* I have used the Reclam edition: G. E. Lessing, *Nathan der Weise: Ein dramatisches Gedicht in fünf Aufzügen* [Nathan the Wise: A dramatic poem in five acts] (Stuttgart: Reclam, 1990), ed. Peter von Düffel, which in turn follows the standard edition: Julius Petersen and Waldemar von Olshausen, eds., *Lessings Werke. Vollständige Ausgabe in fünfundzwanzig Teilen. Teil 2* [Lessing's works: Complete edition in twenty-five parts. Part 2] (Berlin: Bong, 1925).

Lessing wrote *Nathan the Wise* in "blank verse," or unrhymed lines in iambic pentameter. *Iambic* refers to the *iambs,* or two-syllable "feet" with the stress on the second syllable. *Pentameter* refers to the five (Greek: *penta*) instances of *iambs* per line. A famous example of such meter in English literature can be seen in the first two lines of Shakespeare's first sonnet (where the underlined syllables are stressed):

> From <u>fai</u>rest <u>crea</u>tures <u>we</u> de<u>sire</u> in<u>crease</u>
> That <u>there</u>by <u>beau</u>ty's <u>rose</u> might <u>nev</u>er <u>die,</u>

This form adds a musical quality to the language and also carries the advantage of making the lines easier to memorize. Yet such metrical constraints are a nightmare for the translator. Take, for example, the lines the Templar speaks when he first notices the friar watching him:

> Der <u>folgt</u> mir <u>nicht</u> vor <u>langer</u> <u>Weile!</u>—<u>Sieh,</u>
> Wie <u>schielt</u> er <u>nach</u> den <u>Hän</u>den!—<u>Gu</u>ter <u>Bru</u>der, . . .
> Ich <u>kann</u> Euch <u>auch</u> wohl <u>Va</u>ter <u>nen</u>nen; <u>nicht?</u>

One American edition gives the following translation:

> That <u>fel</u>low <u>dogs</u> me <u>not</u> for <u>past</u>ime. <u>See</u>
> How <u>greed</u>i<u>ly</u> he <u>leers</u> u<u>pon</u> my <u>hands</u>!
> Good <u>broth</u>er — <u>or</u> good <u>fath</u>er, <u>poss</u>i<u>bly</u> —[1]

This comes reasonably close to Lessing's meaning, but it is imprecise. The word *folgt* means "follows," not "dogs." The translator chose "dogs" because he needed a one-syllable word. The verb *schielen,* from which the word *schielt* (third person singular) is derived, can mean "to leer," or to watch something furtively or secretly, but Lessing does not use an adverb meaning "greedily" to modify that verb. "Greedily" simply helps to keep the original meter. Nor does the Templar try to call the friar "good father," but simply wants to call him "father." Finally, the translator has transformed a question into a statement to avoid the addition of words such as "can I" or "I can," for which he has evidently run out of space.

Another edition provides the following translation:

> He follows not to pass the time. — And look,
> See how he eyes my hands — My worthy brother . . .
> Or I might call you father, too, no doubt?[2]

This is rather closer to Lessing's meaning. Yet the translator has sacrificed the object of the verb "follows" (that is, "me") because it did not fit into the metrical scheme. Of course, the "me" is implied from the context—there is no one else the friar could be following—but omitting the object results in stilted verse. Moreover, "no doubt" is not an exact translation of *nicht,* which simply means "not," and when combined with the word *kann* ("can") and a question mark calls for something like "can't I?" "No doubt" conveys a sense of confidence that is absent in the original, but the translator apparently used this expression because it lends itself to stress on the second syllable, whereas "can't I" does not sound natural as an iamb and would normally have the stress on the first syllable.

I have chosen to avoid such problems by simply ignoring the metrical rules that Lessing imposed upon himself. Thus, for example, I have taken the above lines and translated them as "This one's not following

---

[1] Gotthold Ephraim Lessing, *Nathan the Wise*, trans. Patrick Maxwell (New York: Bloch Publishing Company, 1923), 159.

[2] Gotthold Ephraim Lessing, *Nathan the Wise, Minna von Barnhelm, and Other Plays and Writings*, ed. Peter Demetz [*Nathan* translation by Bayard Quincy Morgan]. (New York: Continuum, 1991), 191.

me out of boredom! Look how he's trying to steal a glance at my hands! Good brother, . . . I can also call you father, can't I?" I do not claim to have produced what in Leibniz's language would be "the best of all possible translations," but it seems to me that translation is hard enough without adding inflexible structures such as iambic pentameter. Nuances and connotations are frequently lost as it is, and having to reject a reasonable facsimile of an original word or phrase because it has too many or too few syllables only makes matters worse. Purists may argue that I am betraying the original poetry. Here I can comfort myself with the conviction that Lessing wrote *Nathan the Wise* above all to convey a set of meanings, and that meter was of secondary concern to him.

Contents

APPENDIXES

Illustrations

PART ONE

Introduction:
Beyond Tolerance —
Lessing, *Nathan the Wise,*
and the Legacy of
the Enlightenment

LESSING'S CHALLENGE TO CONVENTION

Lessing was a disappointment to his parents. Born on January 22, 1729, in Kamenz, a small town in the German kingdom of Saxony, Gotthold Ephraim Lessing was the eldest son of a Lutheran pastor, who expected the boy to follow in his footsteps and become a preacher of Lutheranism, the official state religion. After completing his secondary studies in 1746, Lessing moved to Leipzig, the capital of Saxony and the site of a great university, where he planned to concentrate in theology. Yet he quickly acquired a preference for more worldly subjects, including medicine. More alarming still, from his parents' point of view, Lessing took an interest in such frivolous pursuits as riding, fencing, dancing, and, worst of all, theater. In the eighteenth century most of European society harbored a prejudice against theater as an immoral activity, and the church especially railed against it. The troupe with which Lessing was associated did not remain long in existence, but after its break-up he moved to Berlin, the capital of neighboring

Prussia and a city notorious for the unorthodox attitudes of many of its inhabitants. The king of Prussia at the time was Frederick the Great, a self-styled *philosophe* or "philosopher" who displayed a marked skepticism toward traditional religion and believed that human happiness came from good government rather than from divine favor. Though Lessing sought to combine his worldly interests with religious principles, he was never happy with what he regarded as the narrow dogmatism of the contemporary Lutheran church and, on the contrary, felt comfortable in the skeptical, freethinking atmosphere of Berlin. There he attempted the difficult task of living by his pen, writing on a wide variety of subjects, including philosophy, theology, and literary and theater criticism. Lessing continued his work as a playwright and in this capacity enjoyed considerable success, though not even his most famous plays could cure his endemic financial ills. It was largely for financial reasons that Lessing worked at a motley assortment of jobs that took him away from Berlin. He served variously as a paid traveling companion to a rich merchant, secretary to an army officer, and librarian. He only felt financially secure enough to start a family at the age of forty-seven, but his domestic happiness turned out to be tragically short-lived. Barely a year after his marriage his wife gave birth to a son who did not survive his first day, and she died two weeks later. Lessing himself only lived another three years. He died on February 15, 1781, shortly after his fifty-second birthday.

Despite his financial troubles, domestic unhappiness, and brief life, however, Lessing produced an impressive body of work. Although he wrote prolifically on many subjects, Lessing was and is still best known for his plays, all of which defied convention in some way. His first major play, *Miss Sara Sampson* (1755), broke with the ancient practice of reserving tragedy for characters of royal or noble birth and vividly depicted the suffering of a middle-class woman who marries against her father's will, feels remorse for doing so, but is poisoned by her husband's former mistress before she and her father can reconcile. Similarly, *Emilia Galotti* (1772) portrays the misery of a young middle-class woman. In this case the title character chooses death when she learns of a prince's plot to rape her, thus suggesting the moral superiority of commoners over those at the top of the social ladder.

Not all of Lessing's plays were tragedies, however. His 1767 play, *Minna von Barnhelm,* is a comedy about a woman who defies convention by taking control of her relationship with a good-hearted but self-pitying army officer and persuading him to marry her despite his embarrassment following a minor scandal in which his honor has

A late 1760s portrait of Lessing, possibly by Georg Oswald May.
Reproduced by permission of Das Gleimhaus, Halberstadt, Germany.

been (falsely) implicated. By ridiculing the excessive attention to "honor" among the upper classes, *Minna* sent an egalitarian message, which was reinforced by its implicit feminism; the play also subtly questioned the worth of the military at a time when officers enjoyed high status in Prussian society.

THE CONDITION OF THE JEWS
IN EIGHTEENTH-CENTURY EUROPE

Prejudice and Discrimination

The play we are concerned with here, *Nathan the Wise,* is also a comedy insofar as it ends happily, although Lessing called it a "dramatic poem," perhaps because it did not follow the typical comedic pattern of ending with a marriage. But the more important convention Lessing defied concerned the traditional depiction of non-Christians. The hero of the play is a Jew, Nathan, whom the very title proclaims "wise"; Muslim characters are similarly portrayed in a sympathetic light. Such respect for Jews and Muslims was a radical departure from tradition. Eighteenth-century writers typically portrayed Jews as greedy moneylenders, depicted Muslims as violent despots and servants of the despots, and represented both religious groups as irrational and fanatical. At the very beginning of the century a professor at the University of Heidelberg, Johann Andrea Eisenmenger, had published a book called *Entdecktes Judenthum* [Jewry Revealed], in which he endorsed centuries-old but entirely fictitious libels accusing the Jews of such atrocities as murdering Christian children and using their blood in religious ceremonies (see Document 1). Islam also suffered abuse from Christian commentators, but few Muslims lived under the jurisdiction of Christians, whereas Jews throughout Europe suffered the consequences of Christian prejudices.

Many territories in Europe banned Jews entirely, and where they were allowed to live they usually had to pay special taxes for the "protection" of a prince or territorial lord, who in turn could revoke this favor or demand higher payment for it at any time. Jews typically had to live in overpopulated ghettos, and although they enjoyed a degree of autonomy in these communities, segregation only reinforced the prejudices of people who almost never had the opportunity to become friends with Jews. Moreover, Jews did not enjoy the right to own land, an important source of livelihood in an economy that was still largely agricultural, nor could they enter most traditional crafts, typically controlled by guilds, which invariably excluded Jews from membership. Universities and academies excluded Jews as well. For most Jews, then, the only unblocked avenues to livelihood were petty commerce and moneylending, activities that brought prosperity to very few in communities that were otherwise quite seriously impoverished. When referring to the Jews, however, many European Christians overlooked the poverty of the vast majority and exaggerated the wealth of the merchants and moneylenders. And since most Christians had only encountered Jews when they needed to borrow money or buy something, their prejudices against them could hardly be expected to disappear.

The Enlightenment and Jewish Emancipation

Even in "enlightened" Prussia under Frederick the Great, the Jews were severely restricted in their liberties. Berlin itself was closed to all but roughly two hundred relatively prosperous Jews whose wealth the monarch considered useful to the kingdom, though even these could be expelled on short notice should their utility expire. Others could only enter the city for one day at a time to sell their wares, and they had to pass through a gate and pay a toll otherwise reserved for the entry of livestock. In 1781 the Prussian reformer Christian Wilhelm von Dohm complained about the Jews' conditions (see Document 2). By this time the Jewish population of Prussia had grown to between 150,000 and 175,000, largely due to the recent Prussian acquisition of Polish lands. These Jews, Dohm argued, could present a threat or a benefit to the Prussian state, depending on how they were treated. Persecution, in his view, was neither morally justified nor politically sound. But Dohm was not the first to denounce discrimination against Jews or the prejudices that served to rationalize it. Fighting religious prejudice was one of the primary goals of the Enlightenment. Historians have long argued over the characteristics of this eighteenth-century movement—and some have even questioned the wisdom of referring to it as a movement at all—but most agree that writers associated with the Enlightenment targeted certain traditions they considered incompatible with reason, nature, or humanity, and that they specifically attacked the tradition of religious intolerance. Toward this end they frequently highlighted the persecution that Jews suffered. In his 1721 novel entitled *Persian Letters,* the French writer Montesquieu included a character who declared, "The Jewish religion is an old trunk that has produced two branches that have covered the entire earth: I mean Mohammedanism [i.e., Islam] and Christianity. It is a mother who has given birth to two daughters, who have covered her with a thousand plagues."[1] In 1748, in a pioneering work of comparative law entitled *Of the Spirit of the Laws,* Montesquieu wrote a fictional "remonstrance" or protest against the Spanish Inquisition, the fearsome Catholic tribunal that still persecuted "heretics" in the eighteenth century. Adopting the perspective of a Jewish protester, the remonstrance included the famous lines, "We follow a religion that you yourselves know God to have cherished once: we think that God still loves it, and you think that he no longer loves it; and since you judge thus, you put to iron and fire those who are in such a pardonable error of believing that God still loves what he loved."[2]

Other Enlightenment writers, including the famous French *philosophe* Voltaire, repeatedly denounced anti-Jewish persecution in the strongest terms. As early as 1714 Voltaire expressed his outrage:

> In Madrid, in Lisbon, [the Inquisitor] lights his fires,
> The solemn bonfires to which the unhappy Jews
> Are sent every year, in pomp, by the priests,
> For not having left the law of their ancestors.[3]

Voltaire did not always show this much sympathy for the Jews, and at times he descended to the expression of prejudices that his own philosophy implicitly repudiated. In his famous novel *Candide,* for example, the Jewish characters are irascible or greedy or both. Elsewhere Voltaire attacked Jews—whom he was otherwise inclined to see as victims of fanaticism—as fanatics themselves. Ironically, even in a poem dedicated to tolerance, Voltaire wrote of the Jews, "though we tolerate them today, if they were masters they could well leave none but our daughters in the world."[4] Despite outbursts of this sort, Voltaire and like-minded *philosophes* implicitly endorsed the equality of Jews and Christians simply by condemning the fanaticism that made invidious distinctions between the two groups.

By the 1780s the implicit question of the Jews' status had become an explicit subject of public discussion. Lessing's *Nathan the Wise,* published two years before Dohm's book, no doubt contributed to the movement for reform in the Jews' status. And in 1782 the Austrian emperor Joseph II, a prominent supporter of the Enlightenment, issued a series of decrees relaxing restrictions on the civil rights of Jews in the kingdoms of Hungary and Bohemia. Although not resulting in full equality, this legislation, known as the *Toleranzpatent,* granted Jews relative freedom of movement and residence, equal access to education, and the freedom to choose their crafts or professions. Soon thereafter writers in France—who regarded their country as the forefront of Enlightenment and did not wish to see it surpassed in this regard—encouraged similar reforms in the French kingdom. In 1785 the Royal Academy of Sciences and Arts in Metz, a city in eastern France with a substantial Jewish minority, sponsored a widely publicized essay contest on the question, "Is there a way of making the Jews more useful and happier in France?"[5] The academy split the prize among three entries, including one written by a Jew, and all three essays were published as books. While differing in specifics, all three essays argued that prejudice and unjust laws prevented Jews from being either happy or useful members of society.[6] The French Revolution of 1789 accelerated the pace of the movement for equality, and although some revolutionaries worried that the Jews were too distinct in their beliefs and practices to become members of the indivisible nation they hoped to create, on September 27, 1791, the revolutionary legislature proclaimed the end to legal distinctions between Jews and non-Jews.[7] What historians call the emancipation of the Jews extended to other countries when French armies conquered neighboring European states and brought revolutionary laws with them, although some of these gains were reversed following the collapse of Napoleon's French empire in 1814 and 1815.

Lessing and Mendelssohn

When arguing for Jewish rights, reformers often invoked the case of the Jewish philosopher Moses Mendelssohn (see Document 4). The son of a poor scribe, Mendelssohn had overcome the effects of poverty, physical disability (he had a humpback), prejudice, and discriminatory laws—he himself had paid the infamous tax on Jews and livestock when first entering Berlin—to become one of Germany's greatest philosophers. After studying the sacred Hebrew texts in the traditional manner, Mendelssohn became convinced that conventional Jewish learning was insufficient for an understanding of the world and of God's intentions for humanity. He consequently turned to non-Jewish philosophers, whose views he sought to synthesize with Judaism. He was particularly influenced by Gottfried Wilhelm Leibniz, whose philosophy of *optimism* claimed that everything occurring in the universe was for the best because everything was part of God's perfect plan (see Document 5). In 1761 the Prussian Royal Academy of Sciences and Literature sponsored an essay contest on the question of whether the principles of theology and morality could be known with scientific certainty, and Mendelssohn's entry won the prize in a highly competitive field that included a philosopher better known to posterity: Immanuel Kant. The details of Mendelssohn's complex argument need not concern us here. Its historical importance lies in its effect on Mendelssohn's contemporaries, who were astonished that a Jew could produce such a work. Shortly after Mendelssohn's death in 1786 the French *philosophe* and future revolutionary Mirabeau published an extended eulogy of the "German Socrates." He wrote, "A man thrown by nature into the midst of a debased horde, born without any kind of fortune, with a weak and even infirm temperament, a timid character, a perhaps excessive mildness ... has risen up into the ranks of the greatest writers that this century has seen born in Germany."[8] Despite this derogatory reference to the Jews as a "debased horde," Mirabeau saw in Mendelssohn proof of the Jews' potential for greatness, asking rhetorically, "Can it not be said that his example ... must reduce to silence those who insist with a quite ungenerous tenacity on depicting the Jews as too debased ever to produce a race of estimable men?"[9] Thus the condition of being "debased" was reversible. Mirabeau implied that if a Jew could rise to greatness under the present circumstances, more Mendelssohns would result from a reform in the Jews' condition.

Mendelssohn was Lessing's friend, chess partner, and philosophical soul mate. Born in the same year (1729), the two men shared a taste for Leibniz's optimism and the conviction that religious differences need not divide humanity. Lessing's admiration for Mendelssohn was such that readers have long seen the Jewish philosopher as the model for Nathan the Wise. In fact, it did not take the phenomenon of Mendelssohn to convince Lessing that Jews were the equals of Christians, though his friendship with the like-minded Jew no doubt strengthened his conviction. In 1749, five years before he met Mendelssohn, Lessing had written a one-act play entitled *The Jews,* in which an anonymous traveler rescues a baron and his daughter from a band of thieves.[10] Only at the end of the play is it revealed that this heroic personage is a Jew. The baron is grateful, but his condescending expression of thanks reveals his general prejudice against Jews: "Oh how respectable the Jews would be if they were all like you!" The Jewish traveler turns the tables on the Christian by replying, "And how worthy of love the Christians would be if they all possessed your features!" Such was the prevalence of anti-Jewish sentiment at the time that the very inclusion of a brave and generous Jew excited controversy. Johann David Michaelis, a professor of philosophy and "oriental languages" (for example, Hebrew and Arabic) at the prominent university of Göttingen, wrote that such a character as the Jewish traveler was "not impossible, but nevertheless all too improbable" since the Jews were, in the professor's view, a "people whose principles, way of life and education" made them regard Christians "with enmity or at least coldly."[11] Unfortunately Michaelis, like many of his contemporaries, was not ready for Lessing's message: Christians do not have a

A 1786 portrait of Moses Mendelssohn.
Reproduced by permission of the Theater Studies Collection, University of Cologne.

monopoly on virtue. In *Nathan the Wise,* Lessing reiterated this message and added a new one: Christians do not have a monopoly on religious truth.

THE PLOT OF *NATHAN THE WISE*

Nathan the Wise is set in Jerusalem at the end of the twelfth century in the midst of the Crusades, that series of religious wars launched by European Christians to conquer Jerusalem from its Muslim rulers. The action begins when Nathan, a wealthy Jew, returns from a voyage and learns that his eighteen-year-old daughter Recha has just barely escaped from a fire in his house. Recha's governess, a Christian woman named Daja, informs Nathan that a Knight Templar (one of the Christian Crusaders) had rescued Recha. Daja, who was widowed when her husband died in the Crusades and wishes to return home, hopes to persuade the Templar to give up his monastic order's vow of celibacy, marry Recha, and take both women back to Europe. Daja has a valuable secret that she is prepared to use in her attempt to convince the Templar: Recha is not Nathan's biological daughter and was baptized before Nathan adopted her. (Recha is not aware of this and considers herself Jewish.) Nathan also encourages the Templar's interest in Recha, though for different reasons. He is grateful to the young man, and Recha is infatuated with him. The Templar is similarly taken with Recha, but marriage plans are interrupted when Sultan Saladin, the Muslim ruler of Jerusalem, sends for Nathan. Saladin, who neglects his own finances, nevertheless worries when his father is in need, and on the advice of his sister Sittah has called on Nathan as a promising source of revenue.

Sittah has advised her brother to embarrass Nathan by asking him which religion he thinks best: Judaism, Christianity, or Islam. Nathan could not claim his own religion as superior without offending the Sultan and could not grant the prize to the Sultan's religion without then abandoning his own. Thus he would be vulnerable to a demand for money to compensate for his inability to provide an answer. When Saladin asks the impossible question, Nathan responds in the form of a parable. He tells of a man who owned a ring that made its wearer "agreeable to God and human beings." The man left the ring to his favorite son as a sign of rulership over the family. This son left it to his favorite son, who in turn did the same. The ring thus remained in the family for many generations, until one heir loved his three sons equally. In moments of weakness he had promised it to each one, and when he was about to die he found himself in a difficult situation. He therefore ordered a jeweler to make two exact copies of the special ring, and he gave each son an identical ring. After his death the sons quarreled. Each claimed to possess the true ring. Nevertheless, "The true ring was indistinguishable . . . almost as indistinguishable as the true religion is to us." The sons, Nathan continues, took their rings to a judge, who recalled that the ring should make its wearer "agreeable to God and human beings." He then asked the sons which of them the other two loved the most. They did not respond, which the judge took as evidence that each son loved himself the most. He consequently suspected that none possessed the true ring. He reasoned that the father had lost the ring and ordered three new ones made to conceal his error. Still, the judge reminded the sons of their father's equal love for them and advised them to behave as though each did have the true ring. They must make themselves agreeable to God and human beings. Then, perhaps many generations hence, the judge concluded, "a wiser man" would make a definitive ruling.

The parable of the rings so impresses and humbles Saladin that he forgets about the money for which he summoned Nathan and only wishes to be his friend. Nathan agrees. He then meets the Templar, who is more enthusiastic than ever about the prospect of marrying Recha. Yet for reasons that only become clear later, Nathan delays in giving his blessing, thus confusing and unintentionally antagonizing the young man. Immediately afterward Daja, who has been waiting in the wings, reveals the secret of Recha's identity to the Templar. Dismayed and indignant, he asks the Patriarch, the head of the church in Jerusalem, what would become of a Jew who adopted a Christian girl and raised her in the Jewish religion. The Patriarch informs him that the punishment would be death by burning and asks whether the Templar knows of such a case. Revolted by the Patriarch's cruelty, the Templar claims that he was only asking a hypothetical question. Yet the Patriarch is suspicious and sends a friar to investigate.

The friar is a good-hearted man and warns Nathan about the Patriarch's suspicions. Yet this is not the first time Nathan and the friar have met. Eighteen years earlier the friar had brought Nathan the infant daughter of Nathan's Christian friend Wolf von Filnek to care for while he was away at war. Wolf died in the fighting, leaving Nathan to decide whether to leave the orphan with Christian guardians or, more scandalously from the Christian perspective, to raise her as his own daughter. Nathan explains why he chose to keep Recha. Just a few days before the baby arrived, his own wife and seven sons had been massacred by Christian Crusaders. Like Job in the Bible, Nathan raged against God but then accepted his "decree." When the friar appeared with the girl, he saw her as God's compensation for the death of his family and believed it his destiny to be her adoptive father.

In the final act surprising information surfaces about the relationship between the principal characters. It turns out that Wolf was the brother of Saladin and Sittah and the father of both Recha and the Templar. Accordingly, Saladin and Sittah are the uncle and aunt of the two young people, who in turn are brother and sister. (Nathan's early suspicion of this relationship explains his prior hesitation to agree to their marriage.) The only person not related to the other major characters by blood is Nathan, but the equally strong bond of affection makes him a viable member of this surprising family. The curtain falls, according to the stage directions, "to silent, repeated hugs from all sides."

NATHAN AND THE PROBLEM OF INTOLERANCE

Nathan the Wise was a scathing indictment of the intolerance that Lessing considered the scourge of his age. Like other Enlightenment writers, Lessing used the plurality of religious faiths to plant the seeds of doubt in the minds of readers about the superiority of Christianity. Montesquieu's *Persian Letters* had attempted this task by featuring fictional Persians who, while traveling in Europe and especially France, comment on what they regard as the strange customs of Christendom. By depicting the "normal" aspects of French life (such as the power of the Pope and the influence of commerce on subjects' lives) as exotic or peculiar, Montesquieu invited readers to hold their beliefs and practices up to critical scrutiny. After all, if not everyone acted and thought as they did, was it necessary that they persist in acting and thinking as they did? At the same time, Montesquieu's travelers identified resemblances between the French and the Persians, although they did so in ways that similarly invited a critical perspective on French culture. For example, the Persians refer to Catholic priests as "dervishes," thus likening them to Muslim mystics under a regimen of strict self-discipline. The implication was that priests were nothing special and certainly not superior to devotees of other religions; they were just another kind of dervish. Finally, the principal character undergoes doubts about the veracity of his own religion, and the counsel he receives from an Imam (prayer leader) is so rigidly dogmatic—he must not stray in the least from the teachings of the theologians—that his skepticism appears justified. Montesquieu thereby encouraged readers to question their own religious assumptions, but in the end Islam does not appear in a favorable light. It is equal to Christianity, though coming from Montesquieu this is hardly a recommendation.

Similarly, Voltaire insisted on the equal worth and truth of Christianity, Judaism, and Islam. Yet for him as well these religions all missed the mark. Voltaire lambasted the Jews of the Old Testament, and occasionally the Jews of his own day, as fanatics who could not live among people with different beliefs. But he largely did this in order to draw attention to the fanaticism he saw in the church. Although his portrayal of Jews and Judaism was informed by numerous factors,[12] it frequently served to embarrass the church by showing the similarities between Christianity and a religion its practitioners often disdained.[13] Voltaire also identified resemblances between Christianity and Islam. In his play *Muhammad, or, Fanaticism* (1742), Voltaire made fanatical Muslims stand allegorically for fanatical Christians, but in the process he disparaged both religions. For Voltaire as for many other *philosophes,* the only true religion was one that was stripped of dogma and traditions and relied exclusively on the natural reason with which God endowed humanity. Christianity, Judaism, and Islam were equal insofar as they departed equally from the true religion. Indeed, an anonymous contemporary work entitled *Treatise of the Three Impostors* argued that Moses, Jesus, and Muhammad had all established false religions by deceiving the gullible populace.[14] Although this author was a pantheist—that is, one who believes that God and nature are the same thing—and Voltaire was not, their conclusions about the three principal monotheistic religions were not far apart. Consequently, Voltaire undermined the tolerance he preached by suggesting that other religions were no better than the Christianity he so disdained. Why, one was permitted to ask, should intolerant religions be tolerated?

Voltaire's answer was that religious tolerance prevented civil war. While in exile in England, Voltaire had been impressed by the multiplicity of religions tolerated in that country. Writing of the London stock exchange, he observed:

> Here Jew, Mohammedan and Christian deal with each other as though they were all of the same faith, and only apply the word infidel to people who go bankrupt. . . . On leaving these peaceful and free assemblies some go to the Synagogue and others for a drink,

this one goes to be baptized in a great bath in the name of Father, Son and Holy Ghost, that one has his son's foreskin cut and has some Hebrew words he doesn't understand mumbled over the child, others go to their church and await the inspiration of God . . . and everybody is happy.

Voltaire added, "If there were only one religion in England there would be danger of despotism, if there were two they would cut each other's throats, but there are thirty, and they live in peace and happiness."[15] This attitude toward organized religion, which many *philosophes* shared, was one of impatient indulgence. Voltaire was *tolerant,* but there is a difference between tolerating something and respecting it. One must keep this in mind when considering the famous tolerance of the Enlightenment.

Even in their most sympathetic portrayals of non-Christians, then, most Enlightenment writers betrayed some annoyance in their persistent adherence to traditional beliefs and practices. Thus Dohm railed against the persecution of the Jews while simultaneously deploring "the sophistic deductions of . . . rabbis." Similarly, in *History of Saladin* (1758), a book that Lessing read while preparing his *Nathan the Wise,* the French writer François-Louis-Claude Marin praised the Muslim leader in the highest terms but showed impatience with his devoutness, writing, "He cultivated a kind of study that was very frivolous and much esteemed by the devout Muslims: that of being familiar with all the Muslim traditions, the explications of the Koran, the different sentiments of the interpreters, the different opinions of the schools; and he took pleasure in disputing on these matters with the priests and Cadhis [religious judges]." (See Document 3.)

Lessing parted ways with most *philosophes* in his approach to religious diversity. Although he shared their practice of juxtaposing Christians and non-Christians, thereby inviting readers to doubt the superiority of their religion, he showed considerably more respect for all three religions than Enlightenment writers typically did. He portrayed the Patriarch as a tyrant and he depicted Daja as a scheming fanatic, but these characters were not true Christians in his view. Lessing's Christian ideal is seen in the humble friar and (eventually) in the Templar, who learns (in more ways than one) how to be a brother. At the same time, Lessing did not consider it necessary to present the non-Christians in an unfavorable light, since he respected their religious beliefs. Although Nathan is a rich businessman and in this respect conforms to a contemporary stereotype, his character is beyond reproach. Nathan cares for people, not money, and there is not the slightest hint of fanaticism in his religious beliefs. Saladin and Sittah likewise display moral excellence. If Sittah is deceptive, it is only to compensate for her brother's reckless generosity and thereby serves to keep the ship of state afloat. Finally, Lessing showed none of Marin's impatience with Saladin's devoutness.

Lessing's respect for the religions in question can be better understood in the context of his philosophy of religion. Despite his quarrels with the established religious authorities of the day, Lessing was deeply religious. Indeed one might say that he quarreled with leaders in the church *precisely because of* his religious convictions. One of his most deeply held convictions was that God did not reveal himself all at once or in the same way to all of humanity, but at different stages of history and in different ways.[16] As with his belief in the philosophy of optimism, Lessing again seems to have owed much to Leibniz. According to Leibniz, the universe was made up of *monads,* conscious beings each of which reflected the universe from a different perspective. Among these monads were human beings, who by their very nature necessarily saw the universe differently from one another. Differing points of view did not mean that one was right and the others were wrong. This *perspectivalism,* or the notion that the truth looks different depending on one's perspective, justified Lessing's belief that even contradictory religions could nevertheless be equally true.[17] Since no human being could comprehend the entirety of God's enormous plan, Lessing reasoned, God had accommodated people by showing them the world according to their ability to perceive it. Religious diversity was therefore not a problem but itself evidence of the divine plan.

This approach to religious diversity is vividly illustrated in Nathan's parable of the rings. There the judge tells the disputing sons—who represent the practitioners of Judaism, Christianity, and Islam—to act as if their rings are authentic, that is, to treat their religious traditions reverently, to think and act in accordance with the principles of piety and morality. He predicts that one day, when humanity is better prepared for knowledge of God, "a wiser man than I will . . . rule" on the dispute of the quarreling brothers. In the meantime, however, and despite their imperfect knowledge of the divine plan, the sons and their descendants should make themselves "agreeable to God and human beings," thus fulfilling the promise of the original ring.

Lessing's advocacy of humility in theological matters is reflected even more clearly in his opinion that humanity will never and *should* never have perfect knowledge of God and creation. Less than a year before the publication of *Nathan,* Lessing wrote, "If God held all truth in his right hand and the sole everlasting urge for truth in his left, with the result that I should be determined to be forever and always mistaken, and said to me, 'Choose,' I would humbly pick the left hand and say, 'Father, grant me that. Absolute truth is for you alone.'"[18] This statement speaks volumes about Lessing's view of religious truth and his theory of humankind. All religious beliefs are limited by the fact that they are *human* beliefs. Human beings may be "always and everlastingly mistaken" about those things that only God can truly know. Yet the "urge for truth" is what makes human beings human, and they should pursue their nature without entertaining the illusion that they can ever attain God's perspective.

Lessing's humility with respect to religious knowledge, his conviction that the quest for truth is nevertheless a quintessentially human activity, and his belief that God revealed himself and his universe to human beings in accordance with their abilities and perspectives all came together in an attitude that went far beyond "tolerance." For many thinkers during the Enlightenment, religious diversity was a necessary evil. For Lessing it was a necessary good.

THE PLAY'S RECEPTION AND RELEVANCE FOR TODAY

In Easter 1779 at the famous book fair in Leipzig, the chief city for publishing in eighteenth-century Germany, 3,000 copies of *Nathan the Wise* were sold. This figure made it the second best-selling book of the decade at the Leipzig fair.[19] Immediately the book provoked controversy. For some readers it was a welcome development. One reviewer in a literary journal praised Lessing for sending the message that practitioners of different religions can please God equally, and another went so far as to impugn the intelligence of critics who disparaged the play. Yet both supporters remained anonymous.[20] Others responded positively to *Nathan* but missed Lessing's point about the harmful nature of prejudice. For example, one reviewer in a journal from Hamburg wrote of Nathan, "He is a Jew, and it will be a joy to all humanitarians if more like him should now emerge from within his nation,"[21] thus echoing the backhanded compliment of the baron to the Jewish traveler in *The Jews:* "Oh how respectable the Jews would be if they were all like you!" And many commentators were overtly hostile. Just as Michaelis could not accept the virtuous protagonist in *The Jews,* many readers of *Nathan* decried Lessing's decision to make a Jew the hero of the story. One reviewer deplored what he viewed as "a satire against the Christian religion," and another reader was so outraged that he wrote a two-volume book attacking it line by line.[22] Other hostile readers responded by writing parodies, such as *Der travestirte Nathan der Weise* [The travestied Nathan the Wise] and *Nathan der Dumme* [Nathan the Stupid], which reinforced the anti-Jewish stereotypes that Lessing had sought to counter.[23]

Moreover, the authorities reacted defensively to the book's publication. *Nathan* was explicitly banned and condemned by government censors in many cities and territories, including Augsburg, Würzburg, Frankfurt, the lands under the control of the Austrian emperor, and Lessing's native Saxony. Officials all gave the same reason: The book constituted an attack on the Christian religion. Indeed, it soon appeared on the *Index Librorum Prohibitorum,* the famous list of books banned by the Catholic Church.[24] As there was no separation of church and state, an attack on the church was an attack on the state.

Under the circumstances, the prospects for staging the play appeared dim. The Hamburg review cited above claimed that *Nathan* could not be brought to the stage because it dealt with "serious truths," which was another way of saying that it was too controversial, and other commentators concurred in this opinion.[25] Lessing himself feared that it would never be performed on stage.[26] A private performance took place in Mannheim in October 1779, but Lessing did not live to see *Nathan* in a public venue. Less than three years after his death, however, Lessing's play was performed publicly. In April 1783 an actor-producer named Theophilius Döbbelin staged it in Berlin, where Frederick the Great held sway and censorship did not affect the controversial work. Döbbelin played the title role himself. This first attempt failed after only three nights, but other producers followed. In the 1780s *Nathan* was performed in the north German city-state of Lübeck and German-speaking theaters in the Austrian-controlled cities of Pressburg (today Bratislava) and Budapest—as of 1781 Joseph II had relaxed the censorship laws—and in 1801 it was staged in Vienna. That same year the great poet Friedrich Schiller made some alterations in the work, deleting roughly a fourth of the dialogue, and Goethe, arguably the most famous German writer ever, directed the revised version in the liberal city of Weimar. This affirmation by the two contemporary giants of German literature prompted a spate of performances elsewhere in Germany.[27]

Throughout the nineteenth century German critics held *Nathan* in high esteem, as they did Lessing's work more generally. With the rise of anti-Semitism in the 1880s, some reverted to the commentary of Lessing's day and criticized the author for portraying a Jew in a favorable light.[28] When Hitler came to power in 1933, the play was not surprisingly banned from schools, lest German students question the official anti-Semitism of the Nazi regime.[29] After World War II *Nathan* returned to the stage and since then has remained one of the most popular theater pieces in the German repertory. Critics have charged that the play provides an easy means for Germans to soothe their consciences in the wake of the Holocaust—the murder by Nazi Germany of six million European Jews—but this criticism seems unfair.[30] Should Germans ignore *Nathan* simply because it presents a message that many of their compatriots failed spectacularly to heed? Besides, it is not only German Gentiles who have found Lessing's message inspiring. Jews in Germany have long admired Lessing and especially appreciated his *Nathan*. Mendelssohn was only the first in a long line of Jews who praised the play. It is especially telling that when an 1812 Prussian law required Jews to take a surname for the purposes of state recordkeeping, many chose the name Lessing.[31]

Moreover, the significance of *Nathan* extends far beyond what Germans and Jews have made of it. Its principal theme—how to reconcile human diversity with the desire for unity—speaks more generally to the human condition. It is therefore not surprising that people of many different religions and nationalities have found its message relevant. A French translation of *Nathan* appeared as early as 1783 and theater-goers even had the opportunity to see it on stage in Paris that same year.[32] Again in the late 1790s, according to one French writer, Lessing was "in vogue in our theaters."[33] In 1810 the writer and political activist Madame de Staël published a book entitled *De l'Allemagne* (On Germany) in which she praised recent German literature, including Lessing's works. She wrote, "The most beautiful of the works of Lessing is *Nathan the Wise:* one finds in no other work religious tolerance put into action more naturally and with more dignity."[34] At least five different French translations were published within the first century after its initial appearance, testifying to the long-standing French interest in the work.

Nathan's work had a similar impact on the English-speaking world. An English translation of *Nathan* was published in 1781, and ten years later a new translation appeared. More than ten new British editions came out during the nineteenth century. In the United States readers relied on these editions until 1868, when a translation by Ellen Frothingham appeared. An enthusiastic reviewer congratulated the publisher for "doing a good work for American culture" by introducing more readers in the United States to a play that "for nearly a hundred years has been teaching in Germany a noble lesson of tolerance."[35] Another reviewer believed that Lessing was particularly relevant to the United States because he "was a modern man," "far in advance of his own age," adding that "[h]is place is with the most enlightened as well as the bravest of our liberal teachers."[36]

By the time this review appeared, in 1868, *Nathan* had already been translated into Dutch, Danish, Swedish, Polish, and modern Greek.[37] Since then it has appeared in Spanish, Italian, Russian, Yiddish, Hebrew, Armenian, Norwegian, and Japanese, among other languages.[38] In recent years the play has been performed on stages around the world, not only in Germany, Austria, France, the United Kingdom, and the United States, but also in Karachi, Pakistan, and Addis Ababa, Ethiopia.[39]

Surprisingly, it has been largely neglected in Israel, where the national theater Habimah staged it only once, in 1966, to a largely indifferent public and overtly hostile theater critics. One Israeli scholar attributed this negative reception to the play's failure to fit into the ideology of Zionism, which emphasizes the persecution of Jews in the Diaspora—the world outside of Israel—in order to make Jewish emigration to Israel seem necessary.[40] Lessing affirmed that people of different religions or nations could, indeed must, learn to live together. He was suspicious of nationalism as a force that unnecessarily divided humanity, as one sees in *Nathan*. Angry over Nathan's perceived coldness to him, the Templar accuses the Jews of arrogance for believing themselves to be the Chosen People. To this Nathan responds, "Neither of us has chosen his people. Are we our people? What does 'people' mean? Are Christians and Jews more Christians and Jews than human beings?" (2, 5) These are uncomfortable questions for Zionism, as they are for any type of nationalism, since they place a higher value on humanity than on the nation or "people" among whom one happens to have been born.

At the same time, Lessing did not wish to erase all differences between people. Critics of the Enlightenment have faulted the *philosophes* for failing to respect human diversity. In their rush to understand "man," so the criticism runs, Enlightenment thinkers failed to appreciate the differences between various kinds of people. In their zeal to achieve the dream of human perfectibility, they mistook their own specific values and practices for universal ideals and became impatient, even hostile, to people who thought or acted differently. Some have even argued that the inability of the Enlightenment to deal with diversity led to a climate in which the Holocaust, the systematic elimination of people considered irredeemably foreign, became possible.[41] This is a heavy burden to lay on the Enlightenment, whose supporters would never have condoned such heinous crimes. Yet precisely because of the atrocities that have been committed in the name of uniformity, it is no longer possible to be uncritical of the tendency, exhibited by many Enlightenment figures, to discount or ignore the fact of human diversity. The difficult task that faces humanity, as moral philosophers have recently noted, is to honor the equality of human beings while acknowledging that they are in significant ways different from one another. The philosopher Zygmunt Bauman has summarized this imperative: "One needs to honour the otherness in the other, the strangeness in the stranger, remembering . . . that it is being different that makes us resemble each other and that I cannot respect my own difference but by respecting the difference of the other."[42] This is precisely where Lessing can help. If many of his contemporaries were impatient with human difference, we can see that Lessing did not share their attitude. His version of the Enlightenment, informed by Leibniz's idea that our differing perspectives are part of the divine plan, valued human difference. This comes through clearly throughout *Nathan,* and in particular at the end of the final scene, where the stage directions call for "repeated hugs from all sides." The play does not end with the various characters tolerating each other. It ends with them embracing each other, and simultaneously embracing their difference from one another. Whether one believes in a divine plan or not, the message of *Nathan the Wise* has never been more relevant than it is today.

NOTES

[1] Charles-Louis de Secondat, baron de Montesquieu, *Lettres persanes* (Amsterdam, 1721; reprint, Paris: F. Roches, 1929), letter 30, 128.

[2] Montesquieu, *De l'esprit des lois* (1755; reprint, Paris: Les Belles Lettres, 1958), book 25, ch. 13, 279–82.

[3] Voltaire, *La Henriade* (1714), in Louis Moland, ed., *Oeuvres complètes de Voltaire* (Paris: Garnier, 1877–1885), vol. VIII, 136.

[4] Voltaire, "Traité sur la tolérance" (1763), in Van den Heuvel, ed., *Mélanges* (Paris: Gallimard, 1961), 627.

[5]*Mercure de France,* February 11, 1786, 69–84; May 26, 1787, 186; December 15, 1787, 131–32; November 7, 1789, 6–11; *Journal de Paris,* no. 187, July 6, 1789, 840–41; and no. 258, September 15, 1789, 1167–68. *Prix proposés, en 1788, par la Société royale des sciences et des arts de Metz, pour les concours de 1789 et 1790* (Metz, 1788).

[6]Thiéry, *Dissertation sur cette question: est-il des moyens de rendre les Juifs plus heureux et plus utiles en France? Ouvrage couronné par la Société royale des sciences et des arts de Metz. Par M. Thiéry, Avocat au Parlement de Nancy* (Paris, 1788); Abbé Henri Grégoire, *Essai sur la régénération physique, morale et politique des Juifs* (Paris, 1789); and *Apologie des Juifs en réponse à la question: est-il des moyens de rendre les Juifs plus heureux et plus utiles en France? Ouvrage couronné par la Société royale des sciences et des arts de Metz. Par Zalkind-Hourwitz, Juif polonois* (Paris, 1789).

[7]For translations of documents relating to debates on Jewish rights in France around the time of the Revolution, see Lynn Hunt, *The French Revolution and Human Rights: A Brief Documentary History* (Boston: Bedford/St. Martin's, 1996), 48–50, 93–101.

[8]Honoré Gabriel Riquetti, comte de Mirabeau, *Sur Moses Mendelssohn, sur la réforme politique des juifs: et en particulier sur la révolution tentée en leur faveur en 1753 dans la grande Bretagne* (London, 1787), 1.

[9]Mirabeau, *Sur Moses Mendelssohn,* 57.

[10]Gotthold Ephraim Lessing, *Die Juden: Ein Lustspiel in einem Aufzuge verfertiget im Jahr 1749* (1749; reprint, Stuttgart: Reclam, 1981).

[11]*Göttingische Anzeigen von Gelehrten Sachen,* June 13, 1754. Article reproduced in Ibid., 50–53.

[12]See Ronald Schechter, *Obstinate Hebrews: Representations of Jews in France, 1715–1815* (Berkeley: University of California Press, 2003), 46–53.

[13]This argument has been made by Peter Gay in *Voltaire's Politics: The Poet as Realist* (Princeton, 1959; reprint, New Haven: Yale University Press, 1988), 351–54; and *The Party of Humanity: Essays in the French Enlightenment* (New York: Knopf, 1964), 103–8.

[14]Abraham Anderson, ed., *The Treatise of the Three Impostors and the Problem of Enlightenment: A New Translation of the Traité des trois imposteurs* (New York: Rowman & Littlefield, 1997). For an excerpt of the *Treatise,* see Margaret Jacob, *The Enlightenment: A Brief History with Documents* (Boston and New York: Bedford/St. Martin's, 2001), 94–114.

[15]Voltaire, *Letters on England,* trans. Leonard Tancock (Harmondsworth: Penguin, 1980), 41.

[16]Lessing, *Die Erziehung des Menschengeschlechts* (Berlin, 1780). For an English translation, see John Dearling Haney, *Lessing's Education of the Human Race* (New York: AMS, 1972).

[17]Henry E. Allison, *Lessing and the Enlightenment: His Philosophy of Religion and Its Relation to Eighteenth-Century Thought* (Ann Arbor: University of Michigan Press, 1966), 121–61.

[18]Letter from Gotthold Ephraim Lessing to his brother Karl, in Karl Lachmann and Franz Muncker, eds., *Gotthold Ephraim Lessings sämtliche Schriften* (Stuttgart: G. J. Göschen, 1866–1924) vol. 13, p. 24.

[19]Hans-Friedrich Wessels, *Lessings "Nathan der Weise": Seine Wirkungsgeschichte bis zum Ende der Goethezeit* (Frankfurt am Main: Athenäum Verlag, 1979), 28–29. The best-selling book was Friedrich Gottlieb Klopstock, *Die deutsche Gelehrtenrepublik* (Hamburg, 1774).

[20]Jo-Jacqueline Eckardt, *Lessing's Nathan the Wise and the Critics, 1779–1991* (Columbia, S.C.: Camden House, 1993), 8.

[21]Review of *Nathan the Wise* from the *Kaiserlich-priviligierte Hamburgische Neue Zeitung* (1779), in Horst Steinmetz, ed., *Lessing—ein unpoetischer Dichter: Dokumente aus drei Jahrhunderten zur Wirkungsgeschichte Lessings in Deutschland* (Frankfurt am Main: Athenäum Verlag, 1969), 109.

[22]Eckardt, 7.

[23] Charlene A. Lea, "Tolerance Unlimited: 'The Noble Jew' on the German and Austrian Stage (1750–1805)," *German Quarterly* 64 (2): 166–77.

[24] Wessel, 30–32, 250.

[25] Wessel, 244–46.

[26] Eckardt, 25.

[27] Wessel, 248–49.

[28] Eckardt, 41–45.

[29] Dominik von König, "'Nathan der Weise' in der Schule: Ein Beitrag zur Wirkungsgeschichte Lessings," *Lessing Yearbook* 6 (1974): 108–38.

[30] Eckardt, 63.

[31] I thank Liliane Weissberg for bringing this to my attention.

[32] Friedel de Bonneville, *Nouveau théâtre allemand,* vol. 7 (N.p., 1783). On the Parisian performance of *Nathan,* see Ursula Schulz, *Lessing auf der Bühne: Chronik der Theateraufführungen 1748–1789* (Bremen and Wolfenbüttel: Jacobi Verlag, 1977), 192.

[33] É[tienne]-J[ean] Delécluze, *Journal* (Paris: 1828; reprint, Paris: Grasset, 1948), 365.

[34] Germaine de Staël, *De l'Allemagne* (1810; reprint, Paris: Hachette, 1958–1960), 268.

[35] "Belles Lettres," in *New Englander and Yale Review* 27 (January 1868): 203, 205.

[36] "Reviews and Literary Notices," *The Atlantic Monthly* (February 1868): 251.

[37] "Belles Lettres," 204; and "Reviews," 250.

[38] *Lessing Yearbook* 32 (2000), passim.

[39] David John, "Lessing, Islam and *Nathan the Wise* in Africa," *Lessing Yearbook* 32 (2000), 245–60.

[40] Gad Kaynar, "Lessing and Non-Lessing on the Israeli Stage: Notes on Some Theological, Political and Theatrical Aspects," *Lessing Yearbook* 32 (2000), 361–70.

[41] Max Horkheimer and Theodor W. Adorno, *Dialectic of Enlightenment,* trans. John Cumming (New York: Continuum, 1988).

[42] Zygmunt Bauman, "Postmodernity, or Living with Ambivalence," in Joseph Natoli and Linda Hutcheon, eds., *A Postmodern Reader* (Albany: State University of New York Press, 1993), 14.

PART TWO

Nathan the Wise

DRAMATIS PERSONAE

SULTAN SALADIN
SITTAH, *his sister*
NATHAN, *a rich Jew in Jerusalem*
RECHA, *his adopted daughter*
DAJA, *a Christian woman, but in the Jew's house as Recha's governess*
A YOUNG KNIGHT TEMPLAR

A DERVISH
THE PATRIARCH OF JERUSALEM
A MONK
AN EMIR[1]
along with various Mamelukes[2] of Saladin

ACT 1

Scene 1

Scene: A hall in Nathan's house. Nathan returning from a voyage. Daja coming toward him.

DAJA: It's him! Nathan! Thank God you're finally back.

NATHAN: Yes, Daja. Thank God! But why do you say "finally"? Was I supposed to come back sooner? Could I have come back sooner? Babylon is a good two hundred miles from Jerusalem, at least by the twisted route I had to take. And collecting debts isn't the sort of business you can do in a hurry.

DAJA: Oh Nathan, how miserable things could have been! Your house . . .

[1]A military governor.
[2]Slave soldiers.

NATHAN: There was a fire. I've already heard about it. God willing, I've already heard everything.

DAJA: It might have burned to the ground.

NATHAN: Then, Daja, we would have built a new one, a nicer one.

DAJA: Yes, of course. But *Recha* was a hair's breadth from being burned to death.

NATHAN: Burned? Who? My Recha? That I hadn't heard. Now then! In that case I wouldn't have needed a house. A hair's breadth from being burned to death! She *is* dead, isn't she? Tell me the truth! Just let it out! Kill me; don't torture me any longer. She's dead.

DAJA: If she were, would you hear it first from me?

NATHAN: Then why did you scare me like that? Oh Recha! My Recha!

DAJA: Yours? Your Recha?

NATHAN: If I ever had to get used to not calling her my child!

DAJA: Do you call everything you have *yours* with equal justification?

NATHAN: Nothing with greater justification! Everything else I have, Nature and Fortune have given me. For this possession alone I have Virtue to thank.

DAJA: Oh, how dearly you make me pay for your goodness, Nathan! If goodness with such intentions can still be called goodness.

NATHAN: With such intentions? With what intentions?

DAJA: My conscience . . .

NATHAN: Daja, let me tell you one thing first of all . . .

DAJA: My conscience . . .

NATHAN: What lovely material I bought you in Babylon. So rich, and so rich in taste! I've hardly brought better material for Recha herself.

DAJA: What does that help when my conscience, I have to tell you, cannot be numbed any longer?

NATHAN: And how you will love the pins, the earrings, the necklaces and rings I brought you from Damascus! I can't wait to see . . .

DAJA: So that's the way you are! If you could do nothing but give gifts! Nothing but give gifts!

NATHAN: Just take as happily as I give—and be quiet!

DAJA: And be quiet! Who would ever doubt, Nathan, that you are honesty, generosity itself? And yet . . .

Above: Ernst Deutsch (1890–1969), a Jewish Austrian actor who fled to the United States to escape the Nazis and returned to Europe after World War II. In 1954 he played Nathan in a German production of the play.

Reproduced by permission of the Theater Studies Collection, University of Cologne.

Right: Actor, playwright, and director August Wilhelm Iffland (1759–1814), a contemporary of Lessing, as Nathan in an 1801 performance of *Nathan the Wise* in Vienna.

Reproduced by permission of the Theater Studies Collection, University of Cologne.

NATHAN: Yet I'm only a Jew. So that's what you want to say?

DAJA: What I want to say, you know better than I do.

NATHAN: Then be quiet!

DAJA: I am quiet. What punishable things in God's eyes are happening here, which I can't stop, can't change, can't . . . it will come back to you!

NATHAN: Come back to me! But then where is she? Where is she? Don't deceive me! Does she know that I've arrived?

DAJA: That I ask you! She's still trembling with fright in every nerve. Her imagination still paints fire on everything it shows her. Her spirit is awake while she sleeps, it sleeps while she's awake: she's sometimes less than an animal, sometimes more than an angel.

NATHAN: Poor child! What are we human beings!

DAJA: This morning she lay a long time with closed eyes, and was like a dead person. Suddenly she awoke and cried, "Listen! Listen! My father's camels are coming! Listen! His own gentle voice!" Then her eyes closed again, and her head, which had been leaning on her arm, fell onto the pillow. I looked past the gate and saw: you really were coming! You really were coming! What a miracle! The whole time her entire soul was only with you — and him.

NATHAN: With him? With whom?

DAJA: With the one who saved her from the fire.

NATHAN: Who was that? Who? Where is he? Who saved my Recha? Who?

DAJA: A young Knight Templar who a few days earlier had been brought here as a prisoner, and who was then pardoned by Saladin.

NATHAN: What? A Templar whom Sultan Saladin left with his life? Recha couldn't have been saved by a lesser miracle? God!

DAJA: Without the one who bet his unexpected winnings again, it would have been the end of her.

NATHAN: Where is this noble man, Daja? Where is he? Lead me to his feet. You must have given him all the treasures I left you, right? Given him everything? Promised him more? Much more?

DAJA: How could we?

NATHAN: No? You didn't?

DAJA: He came, and no one knows from where. He went, and no one knows where. Without the knowledge of anyone in the house, led only by his ear, with his coat spread widely in front of him, he bravely pushed through the flames and smoke after the voice that called to us for help. Just as we gave him up for lost he stood before us, lifting her up with his strong arms. Cold and unmoved by our cheers of thanks, he set his prize down, pushed through the crowd and disappeared!

NATHAN: Not forever, I hope.

DAJA: After a few days we saw him walking back and forth under the palms that shade the grave of the Resurrected One.[3] I approached him with delight, thanked, exalted, summoned, begged—that he would once more see the pious creature who could not rest until she cried out her thanks at his feet.

NATHAN: Well?

DAJA: In vain! He was deaf to our plea, and poured out bitter scorn onto me especially . . .

NATHAN: Until you were scared off . . .

DAJA: Just the opposite! I approached him again every day, let him taunt me every day. What I didn't suffer from him! What I wouldn't have happily endured! But for a long time he hasn't come to visit the palms that shade the grave of the Resurrected One. And no one knows where he's gone. You're surprised? You're thinking?

NATHAN: I'm thinking about what kind of impression that must have made on a mind such as Recha's. To find herself so scorned by the one she feels herself so compelled to revere; to be so repulsed, and yet so attracted. Truly the head and heart must quarrel for a long time before misanthropy or melancholy wins. Often neither wins. And imagination, which intervenes in the quarrel, makes dreamers in whom the head sometimes plays the heart and the heart sometimes plays the head. It's a bad exchange! The latter, if I know Recha, is Recha's case. She's smitten.

DAJA: But she's so pious, so kind!

NATHAN: She's still smitten.

DAJA: She's especially smitten with one idea. It's that her Templar is not of this earth, but of the angels in whose protection her little heart has trusted since childhood; that he came from the cloud that veiled him into the fire that swept around her, and took the form of

---

[3]That is, Jesus.

a Templar. Don't smile! Who knows? At least leave her the illusion in which Jew and Christian and Muslim unite. Such a sweet illusion!

NATHAN: And so sweet to me! Go, honest Daja, go. See how she is, see if I can speak to her. Then I will look for the wild, moody Guardian Angel. And if it still pleases him to linger among us here below, to play the Knight so rudely, I will certainly find him and bring him here.

DAJA: You undertake much.

NATHAN: Then make room next to the sweet illusion for the even sweeter truth. For, Daja, believe me: to a human being another human being is always dearer than an angel. So will you not be angry with me when you see the angel worshipper cured?

DAJA: You are so good, and at the same time so bad! I'm going! But listen, look! Here she comes.

Scene 2

Recha and the previous.

RECHA: Is that you, my father? Is it really you? I thought you'd only sent your voice to me. Why do you hesitate? What mountains, what deserts, what streams still separate us? I can feel your breath, but you're not hurrying to embrace your Recha, who meanwhile burned to death! Nearly, nearly burned to death! Just nearly. Don't shudder! It's a nasty way to die, burning. Oh!

NATHAN: My child! My dear child!

RECHA: You had to cross the Euphrates, Tigris, Jordan, who knows how many waters altogether? How often the thought made me quiver before fire came so close to me. But since the fire came so close to me dying in water seems delightful, refreshing, salvation. But you haven't drowned and I, I haven't burned. We must rejoice and praise God! He, he carried you and your boat across the fickle streams on the wings of *invisible* angels. He, he made my angel *visible*, so I saw his white wings as he carried me through the fire.

NATHAN: [*Aside:* White wings! Yes, yes! The waving white coat of the Knight Templar.]

RECHA: Visibly, visibly he carried me through the fire, his wings waving. In this way I, I saw an angel face to face. And *my* angel.

NATHAN: Recha would be worth it. And she would see nothing more beautiful in him than he would in her.

RECHA: [*smiling*] Whom are you flattering, my father? The angel, or yourself?

NATHAN: But if only a human being, a human being as nature makes every day, had rendered you this service, he should be an angel to you. He should and he would.

RECHA: Not that kind of angel. No! A real one. It was truly a real one! Didn't you yourself teach me of the possibility that it is through angels that God does good, even miracles, to those who love him? Did you not teach me that he can do miracles? And I love him truly.

NATHAN: And he loves you. And every hour he does miracles for you and your fellow creatures. Yes, he has always done that for you.

RECHA: I like to hear that.

NATHAN: Why? Just because it would sound really natural, really ordinary, if an actual Templar had saved you, should it therefore be any less of a miracle? The greatest miracle is that the true, genuine miracles can and should become ordinary. Without this general miracle, a thinking person would hardly use the word "miracle" to describe those things that seem miraculous to children, who with open mouths stare only at the most unusual and the newest things.

DAJA: [*to Nathan*] Do you want to explode her already overstressed brain with such subtleties?

NATHAN: Leave me be! Wouldn't it be enough of a miracle to my Recha that a *man* saved her, who by no small miracle had just been saved himself. Yes, no small miracle! For who has ever heard of Saladin sparing a Templar? Of a Templar ever asking or hoping to be spared? Ever offering him for his freedom more than the leather belt that bears his sword; and at the most his dagger?

RECHA: That proves it to me, my father. Precisely for that reason it could not have been a Templar. It only seemed to be. No imprisoned Templar could ever come to Jerusalem without coming to certain death. Yet no one goes so freely around Jerusalem. How could such a man have voluntarily saved me at night?

NATHAN: See? How sensible. Now, Daja, say something. I have it from you that he was sent here as a prisoner. Without a doubt you know more.

DAJA: Well, yes. That *is* said. At the same time it is said that Saladin pardoned the Templar because he so greatly resembled a brother he especially loved. But as it has been more than twenty years since this brother has been dead—I don't know what his name was, I don't know where he was—it sounds so very, so very unbelievable, that the whole thing probably just isn't true.

NATHAN: But Daja! Why should that be so unbelievable? And not because—as sometimes happens—you want to believe something even more unbelievable? Why should Saladin, who in general loves his brothers and sisters so much, not have been able in his younger years to have a special love for one of his brothers? Don't two faces ever resemble one another? Is an old impression necessarily lost? Does it no longer have the same effect? Since when? What part of this is unbelievable? And indeed, wise Daja, would this no longer be a miracle to you? And only *your* miracles have . . . deserve, I would like to say, to be believed.

DAJA: You're mocking me.

NATHAN: Because you mock me. Still, Recha, your rescue remains a miracle, only possible for Him who likes to guide the most serious decisions, the most outlandish plans of kings, with the weakest threads. That's his game, if not his mockery.

RECHA: My father! My father, if I'm wrong, you know, I don't like to be wrong.

NATHAN: Even more, you like to learn. Look! A forehead, arched this way or that. The curve of a nose leading this way or that. Eyebrows that slither this way or that on a sharp or dull bone; a line, a joint, a corner, a fold, a something, a nothing, on a wild European's face . . . and you escape a fire, in Asia! Isn't that a miracle, miracle-greedy people? Why should you trouble an angel?

DAJA: What harm does it do—Nathan, if I may speak—in all this to prefer to think you've been saved by an angel instead of a man? Wouldn't you feel that much closer to the first incomprehensible cause of your salvation?

NATHAN: Pride! And nothing more than pride! The iron pot wants to be pulled out of the fire by silver tongs in order to fancy itself a pot of silver. Bah! And what harm does it do, you ask. What harm does it do? What good does it do, I should like to ask. For your "feeling so much closer to God" is nonsense or blasphemy. It only harms; yes, it really harms. Come! Listen to me. Isn't it true that for this being that saved you—whether it is an angel or a man—that for this being you two, and you especially,[4] would wish to do great services? Isn't it so? Now, for an angel, what services, what great services could you do? You could thank him. You could sigh to him, pray to him. You could melt in delight over him. On his holiday you could fast, give alms.[5] All nothing! For it seems to me still that only you and your companion profit more from all this than he does. He won't get fat from your fasting, won't get rich from your charity, won't become more glorious from your delight, won't grow more powerful from your trust. Isn't it so? But if he's a man . . .

DAJA: But a man would have given us more of an opportunity to *do* something for him. And God knows how ready we would have been for this! But he so fully wanted, needed nothing, was in himself, so content with himself, as only angels are, as only angels can be.

RECHA: Finally, when he just disappeared . . .

NATHAN: Disappeared? What do you mean, disappeared? Was no longer to be seen among the palms? How? Or have you really already looked for him?

DAJA: Now we haven't done that.

NATHAN: No, Daja? No? Now you'll see what harm it does! Cruel worshippers! What if this angel were now—now sick!

RECHA: Sick!

DAJA: Sick! He can't be!

RECHA: What cold shivers have overcome me! Daja! My forehead, normally so warm, feel! It's suddenly ice.

NATHAN: He's a Frank,[6] not used to this climate. He's young, not used to the hard work of his order, not used to hunger, to watches.

RECHA: Sick! Sick!

DAJA: Only Nathan thinks it possible.

NATHAN: He's lying there now! Has neither friends nor money to attract friends.

RECHA: Ah, my father!

---

[4]Nathan means Recha.
[5]Nathan is referring to the custom of celebrating saints' days.
[6]A term generally used to identify people coming from the area that corresponds to modern Germany.

NATHAN: Lying without help, without advice or encouraging words, prey to pain and death there!

RECHA: Where? Where?

NATHAN: He, who threw himself into the fire for someone he'd never known or seen—it was enough that she was a human being . . .

DAJA: Nathan, be gentle to her!

NATHAN: He who, to spare her the obligation of thanking him, didn't want to know or see the one he saved . . .

DAJA: Spare her, Nathan!

NATHAN: Didn't ask to see her again, unless he should have to save her a second time—it's enough that she's a human being.

DAJA: Stop and look!

NATHAN: He who, dying, has nothing to comfort himself with but the consciousness of this deed!

DAJA: Stop! You're killing her!

NATHAN: And you've killed him! You could have killed him. Recha! Recha! It's medicine, not poison, that I'm giving you. He's alive! Wake up! He's probably not even sick, not even sick!

RECHA: Really? Not dead? Not sick?

NATHAN: Really, not dead! For God still rewards good deeds done here. Oh Recha! But don't you understand how much easier *pious worship* is than *doing good*? How happily the laziest person just piously worships—though he's sometimes unaware of the goal— to avoid having to do good?

RECHA: Ah, my father! Never, never leave your Recha alone again! Isn't it so, he might be traveling.

NATHAN: Oh come on, of course not. But I see over there a Muslim is curiously inspecting my loaded camels. Do you know him?

DAJA: Ha! Your dervish.[7]

NATHAN: Who?

DAJA: Your dervish, your chess partner!

NATHAN: Al-Hafi? Is that Al-Hafi?

DAJA: Now the Sultan's treasurer.

NATHAN: What? Al-Hafi? Are you dreaming again? It's him! It's really him! He's coming. Go inside, you two! I wonder what I'll hear.

---

[7]A dervish is an ascetic and mystical Muslim.

Scene 3

Nathan and the dervish.

DERVISH: Open your eyes, why don't you, as wide as you can!

NATHAN: Is that you, or isn't it? In such splendor, a dervish! . . .

DERVISH: Well, why not? Can't a dervish become anything, anything at all?

NATHAN: Oh yes, of course, certainly! It's just that I always thought the dervish, the true dervish, wouldn't ever want to become anything but a dervish.

DERVISH: By the Prophet![8] That I'm not a true dervish may well be. But when you have to . . .

NATHAN: Have to! A dervish! A dervish has to? No one has to have to, but a dervish has to?[9] What does he have to do?

DERVISH: What he's asked to do and thinks is good: that's what a dervish has to do.

NATHAN: By our God! You've truly said it. Let me hug you, man. You're still my friend?

DERVISH: Shouldn't you first ask what I've become?

NATHAN: Despite what you've become!

DERVISH: And what if I'd become a guy who works for the state and whose friendship was awkward for you?

NATHAN: If you're still a dervish in your heart, I'll risk it. The guy who works for the state is nothing but his uniform.

DERVISH: Which also deserves respect. What do you think? Guess! What would I be at your court?

NATHAN: A dervish; nothing else. Though on the side, probably, a cook.

DERVISH: Well then! And unlearn my trade with you. A cook! Not a waiter too? Admit that Saladin knows me better. I've become his treasurer.

NATHAN: You? His?

DERVISH: Admittedly only for his smaller treasury, since his father still manages the larger one. His household treasury.

---

[8]An oath referring to the Prophet Muhammad (570–632), the founder of Islam.

[9]The German original is literally, "No human being must must, and a dervish must?" *(Kein Mensch muss müssen, und ein Derwisch müsste?)*

NATHAN: His household is big.

DERVISH: And bigger than you think, since every beggar belongs to his household.

NATHAN: But Saladin hates beggars so much . . .

DERVISH: That he sets out to get rid of them, even if he has to become a beggar himself.[10]

NATHAN: Splendid! That's just what I mean.

DERVISH: He is splendid, except for one thing! Every day at sunset his treasury is much emptier than empty. The wave that comes so high in the morning is long gone by afternoon.

NATHAN: Because canals devour, and to fill or to stop them is equally impossible.

DERVISH: Exactly!

NATHAN: I'm familiar with that!

DERVISH: Of course there's little left when princes are vultures in the midst of carrion, but when they're carrion in the midst of vultures there's ten times less.

NATHAN: But no, dervish! No!

DERVISH: That's easy for you to say! Tell me, what will you give me if I give you my job?

NATHAN: What does your job bring you?

DERVISH: Me? Not much. But you, you could really profit from it.[11] If there's an ebb in the treasury, as there often is, you just open your flood-gates: offer an advance and take whatever interest you like.

NATHAN: And interest on interest on interest?

DERVISH: Of course!

NATHAN: Until my capital is nothing but interest.

DERVISH: That doesn't tempt you? Then write the divorce letter for our friendship! Since I was truly counting on you.

NATHAN: Truly? Why then? Why?

---

[10]Saladin enjoyed a reputation for being extraordinarily generous in giving charity. Cf. Document 3.

[11]Lessing uses the verb *wuchern,* which comes from the noun *Wucher,* or usury. He thereby alludes to the prejudice according to which Jews were especially susceptible to usury, or the charging of excessive interest on loans; yet Nathan responds by ridiculing the practice, thus undermining the prejudice.

DERVISH: To help me fulfill my office with honor, your purse would always be open to me. You're shaking your head?

NATHAN: Now we understand each other! Here's the difference. You? Why not you? Al-Hafi the dervish is always welcome to everything I have. But Al-Hafi the defterdar[12] to the Sultan, who, whom—

DERVISH: As I suspected. That you were always as good as you were clever, as clever as you were wise! Patience! What you distinguish in Al-Hafi will soon be separated again. See this honorable costume that Saladin gave me. Before it fades, before it turns to rags, the proper clothing of a dervish, hang it on a hook in Jerusalem, and I'll be on the Ganges,[13] where I'll walk lightly and barefoot on the hot sand with my teachers.

NATHAN: That's more like you!

DERVISH: And play chess with them.

NATHAN: Your favorite thing!

DERVISH: Just think what led me astray! So that I myself could no longer beg? So that I could play the rich man with beggars? That I would be able to make a rich beggar into a poor rich man in a flash?

NATHAN: Certainly not that.

DERVISH: Something much more tasteless! For the first time I felt flattered, flattered by Saladin's goodhearted madness . . .

NATHAN: Which was?

DERVISH: "Only the beggar could know how a beggar feels; only a beggar would have learned the right way to give to beggars. Your predecessor," he said, "was too cold, too raw. He gave so ungraciously when he gave; first inquired so vehemently into the situation of the receiver; never satisfied that he was lacking, also wanted to know the cause of the lack, in order to measure the cause stingily against the offering. Al-Hafi wouldn't do that! He would never show himself so reluctantly charitable to Saladin! Al-Hafi isn't like clogged pipes that take clear and still water and return it dirty and bubbling. Al-Hafi thinks; Al-Hafi feels as I do!" So lovely the bird-catcher's pipe sounded, until the foolish bird was in the net. What an arrogant fool I've been! A fool's fool!

---

[12] Persian for treasurer.
[13] A major river in India, sacred to Hindus (though not to Muslims).

NATHAN: Easy, my dervish, easy!

DERVISH: What? It wouldn't be foolishness to oppress, impoverish, plunder, torment, strangle; and to want to appear as a philanthropist to a few? It wouldn't be foolishness to mimic the gentleness of God, who without prejudice spreads himself over good and evil and plain and desert, in sunshine and rain, and not always to have God's full hand? Well? Wouldn't it be arrogance . . .

NATHAN: Enough! Stop!

DERVISH: Just let me mention *my* arrogance! Well? Wouldn't it be arrogance all the same to track down the positive side of such arrogance in order to take part, for the sake of this positive side, in this arrogance? Well? Wouldn't it be?

NATHAN: Al-Hafi, see to it that you get back to your desert. I'm afraid that especially among human beings you might forget how to be a human being.

DERVISH: Right, I fear that too. Farewell!

NATHAN: So hasty? But wait, Al-Hafi. Will the desert run away from you? Just wait! If only he heard me! Hey, Al-Hafi! Here! He's gone; and I would have liked so much to ask him about our Templar. Presumably he knows him.

Scene 4

Daja coming quickly. Nathan.

DAJA: Oh Nathan, Nathan!

NATHAN: Well? What is it?

DAJA: It's him again! It's him again!

NATHAN: Who, Daja? Who?

DAJA: Him! Him!

NATHAN: Him? Him? When do you not see *Him?* Oh yes, only your him is called "Him." That shouldn't be! Not even if he were an angel![14]

DAJA: He's walking again back and forth among the palms; and from time to time he breaks off dates.

NATHAN: He eats? A Templar?

---

[14]Nathan implies that Daja is confusing the Templar with *Him,* i.e., God.

DAJA: Why are you tormenting me? Her curious eye already saw him behind the thick palm grove, and followed him carefully. She asks you—begs you—to approach him immediately. Oh hurry! She'll wave to you from the window to let you know if he's coming nearer or going farther away. Oh hurry!

NATHAN: Like this, having just come down from a camel? Is that good form? Go, hurry to him and tell him I've returned. Mind you, it was only in my absence that the worthy man didn't want to enter my house; he wouldn't be averse to coming when the father himself has him invited. Go, tell him that I ask him, sincerely ask him . . .

DAJA: All in vain! He wouldn't come to you, since, in short, he wouldn't come to any Jew.

NATHAN: So go, at least go and stop him; at least to keep an eye on him. Go, I'll come after you soon.

[*Nathan hurries inside, and Daja outside.*]

Scene 5

Scene: A square with palm trees, under which the Knight Templar walks back and forth. A friar follows him at some distance from the side, always looking as if he wants to speak with him.

TEMPLAR: This one's not following me because he's bored! Look how he's trying to steal a glance at my hands![15] Good brother, . . . I can also call you father, can't I?

FRIAR: Just brother, just a lay brother; at your service.

TEMPLAR: Yes, good brother, if I only had something to give! By God! By God! I have nothing.

FRIAR: And yet thank you kindly! May God give you a thousand times what you would like to give. For it's the will, not the gift, that makes the giver. But I wasn't at all sent to you to ask for alms, sir.

TEMPLAR: But you were sent?

FRIAR: Yes, from the monastery.

TEMPLAR: Where I was just hoping to find a small pilgrim's meal?

FRIAR: The tables were already taken; but you should just come back with me, sir.

---

[15]The friar belongs to a mendicant order, that is, a congregation that relies on charity, and is thus presumably expecting alms.

TEMPLAR: What for? I've gone a long time without eating meat: but what's the difference? The dates are ripe.

FRIAR: You should beware of this fruit, sir. It's not good to eat too many; they clog the spleen; make your blood melancholic.[16]

TEMPLAR: And if I'd like to feel melancholic? But it wasn't for this warning that you were sent to me, was it?

FRIAR: Oh no. I'm supposed to find out about you; sound you out.

TEMPLAR: And you tell me that yourself?

FRIAR: Why not?

TEMPLAR: [*Aside:* A crafty brother!] Are there more like you in the monastery?

FRIAR: Don't know. I must obey, sir.

TEMPLAR: And yet you obey without much questioning?

FRIAR: Would it otherwise be obeying, sir?

TEMPLAR: [*Aside:* It's true that simplicity is always right!] But could you let me in on who wants to know me better? That it isn't you, I could swear.

FRIAR: Would that be proper? Would it be of any use to me?

TEMPLAR: To whom is it proper and of any use to be so curious? To whom?

FRIAR: To the Patriarch, I must believe. For he sent me to you.

TEMPLAR: The Patriarch? Doesn't he know the red cross on the white cloak any better than that?

FRIAR: But I recognize it!

TEMPLAR: Well, brother? Well? I am a Templar, and a prisoner. And what's more: taken prisoner at Tebnin,[17] the castle we would have gladly climbed in the final hour of the cease-fire in order to fire on Sidon;[18] and what's more: of twenty prisoners Saladin pardoned only me. Now the Patriarch knows what he needs to know—more than he needs.

---

[16]According to the long-popular theory of the Greek physician Galen (ca. 130–ca. 200 C.E.), an excess of black bile (Greek: *melancholia*) led to mental disorders. The Templar's reply refers to the everyday sense of melancholy as simply sad.

[17]A fortress in Lebanon, captured by Saladin in 1187.

[18]A major port city in Lebanon.

FRIAR: But hardly more than he already knows. He would also like to know why Saladin pardoned you, sir, and you alone.

TEMPLAR: Do I know that myself? My neck already bared, I kneeled on my cloak, waiting for the blow, when Saladin looked me closer in the eye, jumped closer to me and waved. I'm lifted up, unchained; want to thank him; see tears in his eyes. He's mute, so am I. He goes, I stay. How that all fits together let the Patriarch himself figure out.

FRIAR: He figures that God must have preserved you for great, great things.

TEMPLAR: Yes, for great things! To save a Jewish girl from a fire; to accompany curious pilgrims to Mount Sinai; and other such things.

FRIAR: Great things will certainly come! What you've done already is not so bad. Perhaps the Patriarch himself already has much more important business for you, sir.

TEMPLAR: So? You mean, brother...? Has he already let you know what it is?

FRIAR: Oh yes indeed! I'm supposed to examine you, sir, to see if you're really the man for the job.

TEMPLAR: Alright, go ahead and examine! [*Aside:* I'd like to see how this one examines!] Well?

FRIAR: The quickest way is to reveal the Patriarch's wishes quite directly to you, sir.

TEMPLAR: Good!

FRIAR: He would like you to send a note for him, sir.

TEMPLAR: Me? I'm not a messenger. This, this is the task that's supposed to be so much more glorious than pulling a Jewish girl from the fire?

FRIAR: But it must be! For, the Patriarch says, this note is of great importance to all of Christendom. Whoever delivers this note, the Patriarch says, will be rewarded by God with a very special crown as soon as he gets to Heaven. And no one would be worthier of this crown, the Patriarch says, than you, sir.

TEMPLAR: Than I?

FRIAR: For there is hardly anyone more capable of earning this crown, the Patriarch says, than you, sir.

TEMPLAR: Than I?

FRIAR: You would be free here, could look around everywhere; you know how to storm and protect a city; you could, the Patriarch says, best judge the strengths and weaknesses of Saladin's newly built inner second wall, describe them most clearly, the Patriarch says, to the warriors of God.

TEMPLAR: Good brother, if I only knew better the contents of the note.

FRIAR: Yes that, that I don't know so well myself. But the note is to King Philip.[19] The Patriarch ... I've often wondered how such a saint, who otherwise lives so fully in Heaven, at the same time can be bothered to be so well informed of the things of this world. It must get annoying to him.

TEMPLAR: Well then? The Patriarch?

FRIAR: Knows quite exactly, quite reliably, how and where, how strongly, from which side Saladin will open his campaign, in case the fighting starts again in earnest.

TEMPLAR: He knows that?

FRIAR: Yes, and would very much like to let King Philip know it, so that he can measure whether the danger would really be so terrible to justify restoring, cost what it will, the cease-fire with Saladin,[20] which your order so bravely violated.

TEMPLAR: What a Patriarch! Well then! The dear, brave man doesn't want me as a common messenger; he wants me as a spy. Tell your Patriarch, good brother, explaining my reasons to the best of your abilities, that this isn't to my taste. I still have to see myself as a prisoner; and the Templar's only calling is to thrust forward with the sword, not to be a spy.

FRIAR: Just as I thought! I don't really blame you, sir. But the best is yet to come. The Patriarch has also figured out the name and location in Lebanon of the stronghold where all the enormous sums of money are hidden that Saladin's careful father uses to pay the army and to defray the expenses of preparation for war. From time to time Saladin makes his way to this stronghold on remote paths, and hardly accompanied. You understand, don't you?

TEMPLAR: By no means!

FRIAR: What would be easier than to seize Saladin? To finish him off?

[19] Philip II (1165–1223), king of France and one of the leaders of the Third Crusade.
[20] A reference to the cease-fire of 1192.

You're shuddering? Oh, a few God-fearing Maronites[21] have already offered to do the deed, if only a valiant man would lead them.

TEMPLAR: And the Patriarch has chosen me as this valiant man?

FRIAR: He thinks that in this matter King Philip could best lend a hand from Ptolemais.[22]

TEMPLAR: To me? To me, brother? Me? Haven't you heard, just heard, what kind of obligation I have to Saladin?

FRIAR: Certainly I've heard.

TEMPLAR: And still?

FRIAR: Yes—the Patriarch thinks—that may be, but God and the orders . . .

TEMPLAR: Change nothing! Don't ask me to be a rogue!

FRIAR: Certainly not! Only, the Patriarch thinks, if you are a rogue to human beings you are not necessarily a rogue to God.

TEMPLAR: I owe my life to Saladin, and I should rob him of his?

FRIAR: Oh come on! But Saladin, the Patriarch thinks, still remains an enemy of Christendom and can't claim any right to be your friend.

TEMPLAR: Friend? A man to whom I just don't want to become a scoundrel, an ungrateful scoundrel?

FRIAR: Of course! Still, the Patriarch thinks, when it comes to gratitude we're even, even before God and human beings, if the action is not committed for our sake. And since it's been said, the Patriarch thinks, that Saladin only pardoned you because something in your face, in your being reminded him of his brother . . .

TEMPLAR: This the Patriarch knows as well, and still? Ah! If this were certain! Ah, Saladin! What? Nature should have put just *one* of my features in your brother's form, without this corresponding to anything in my soul? What this corresponded to, could I suppress it to please a Patriarch? Nature, you don't lie like this! Nor does God contradict himself in his work! Go, brother! Don't make me angry! Go! Go!

FRIAR: I'm going, and happier than when I came. Pardon me, sir. We monastic people are obligated to obey our superiors.

---

[21]Maronites were originally Syrian Christians separate from the Roman church. In the late twelfth century they joined with Rome and supported the Crusades.

[22]A city, also known as Acre or Acco, on the bay of Haifa (today Israel). It was the main stronghold of the Crusaders.

Scene 6

The Knight Templar and Daja, who for awhile has been observing the Templar from afar and now approaches him.

DAJA: It seems the friar didn't leave him in the best mood. Still I have to take my chances.

TEMPLAR: Well, splendid! Does the proverb lie: that monk and woman, and woman and monk are both the devil's claws? Today he's thrown me from the one into the other.

DAJA: What do I see? Noble knight, is it you? Thank God! A thousand thanks to God! Where have you been hiding all this time? You haven't been ill, have you?

TEMPLAR: No.

DAJA: You're healthy then?

TEMPLAR: Yes.

DAJA: We were really very concerned about you.

TEMPLAR: So?

DAJA: You must have been traveling, right?

TEMPLAR: Good guess!

DAJA: And just came back?

TEMPLAR: Yesterday.

DAJA: Recha's father also arrived today. And now may Recha hope?

TEMPLAR: For what?

DAJA: For what she has so often begged of you. Her father himself will soon beg you to come. He's returned from Babylon. With twenty heavily laden camels, and everything precious that India and Persia and Syria, even China have to offer in stones and cloths.

TEMPLAR: I'm not buying anything.

DAJA: His people worship him as a prince. But I've often been amazed that they call Nathan "the Wise" rather than "the Rich."

TEMPLAR: Perhaps rich and wise are the same thing to his people.

DAJA: Above all they should have called him "the Good." For you can't imagine how good he is. When he learned how much Recha owes you, what he wouldn't have given you, done for you at that moment!

TEMPLAR: Ah!

DAJA: Give him a try, come and see!

TEMPLAR: What? How quickly a moment passes?

DAJA: If he weren't so good, would I have agreed to stay with him for so long? Do you think I somehow don't feel my worth as a Christian? And it wasn't sung over my cradle that I would follow my husband to Palestine only to raise a Jewish girl. My dear husband was a noble knight in Emperor Frederick's army—

TEMPLAR: A Swiss by birth, who had the honor and grace to drown in a river with His Imperial Majesty.[23] Woman! How many times have you already told me that? Won't you ever stop pursuing me?

DAJA: Pursuing! Dear God!

TEMPLAR: Yes, yes, pursuing. I never want to see you again! Don't want to hear you! Don't want to be reminded again and again of a deed that I did without thinking about it; that, when I think about it, is a mystery to me. Of course I don't want to regret it. But look; if such a case happens again, it's your fault if I don't act so quickly, if I look into things first—and let burn what's burning.

DAJA: God forbid!

TEMPLAR: From now on just do me this one favor and act as if you don't know me. I beg you. And keep the father away from me too. A Jew is a Jew. I'm just an ordinary Swabian.[24] The girl's image disappeared long ago from my mind, if it was ever there in the first place.

DAJA: But yours isn't gone from hers.

TEMPLAR: So what's it doing there? What?

DAJA: Who knows! People aren't always what they appear to be.

TEMPLAR: But they're seldom any better. [*He goes.*]

DAJA: But wait! What's the hurry?

TEMPLAR: Woman, don't make me hate the palms that I normally like so much to walk under.

DAJA: Then go, you German bear! Go!—And yet I mustn't lose track of this animal. [*She follows him from a distance.*]

---

[23]Emperor Frederick I, "Barbarossa" (1123–1190), was a Crusade leader who drowned while on campaign.

[24]The inhabitants of Swabia, a state in southwestern Germany, had the reputation of being simple and unsophisticated.

ACT 2

Scene 1

Scene: The Sultan's palace.

Saladin and Sittah are playing chess.

SITTAH: Where are you, Saladin? How you're playing today!

SALADIN: Not well? I thought I was.

SITTAH: For me you are, but barely. Take this move back.

SALADIN: Why?

SITTAH: Your knight is unprotected.

SALADIN: That's right. Well, then!

SITTAH: Then I'll have you in a fork.

SALADIN: Right again. Check then!

SITTAH: What does that help you? I'll move here, and you're right back where you were.

SALADIN: I can see very well that I'm not getting out of this trap without paying for it. Oh well! Just take the knight.

SITTAH: I don't want it. I'll go past it.

SALADIN: You're not giving me anything. There's more for you in this plan than the knight.

SITTAH: Perhaps.

SALADIN: Don't reckon without your host. Look at this! Admit it, you wouldn't have suspected this.

SITTAH: Of course not. How could I have suspected that you were so tired of your queen?

SALADIN: Of my queen?

SITTAH: Now I see: I should win my thousand dinars[25] today, not a penny more.

SALADIN: Why?

SITTAH: You have to ask! Because you're making every effort to lose. But this isn't what I'd counted on. Besides the fact that such a game is hardly entertaining: haven't I always won the most from you when I lost? When haven't you given me twice the stakes I owed you for a lost game just to console me?

---

[25] A dinar was a gold coin circulating in Islamic states from the seventh century.

SALADIN: See? So when *you* have lost, you've made every effort to do so, dear sister, right?

SITTAH: At least I can say that your generosity, my dear brother, is responsible for the fact that I haven't learned to play better.

SALADIN: We're getting away from the game. Finish!

SITTAH: So it's staying this way? Well then: check! And double check!

SALADIN: Well now! I hadn't seen that with this check I'll lose my queen.

SITTAH: Could that be helped? Let's see.

SALADIN: No, no; just take the queen. I was never very happy with that piece.

SITTAH: Just with that piece?

SALADIN: Get on with it!—That doesn't hurt me. Now everything is protected again.

SITTAH: My own brother taught me how to be polite to queens. [*She leaves it standing.*]

SALADIN: Take her or don't take her! Either way I don't have her.

SITTAH: Why take her? Check!—Check!

SALADIN: Keep going.

SITTAH: Check!—and check!—and check!

SALADIN: And mate!

SITTAH: Not quite. Move the knight between these pieces, or whatever you want. It's all the same.

SALADIN: Quite right! You've won: and Al-Hafi will pay you. Have him called! Quickly! Sittah, you weren't so wrong; I wasn't so completely in the game, I was distracted. And then: who keeps giving us these smooth stones, which don't remind us of anything, don't signify anything? Was I playing with the Imam?[26] Oh, well. Loss calls for an excuse. It's not the formless pieces, Sittah, that made me lose: it's your skill, your calm and quick glance . . .

SITTAH: Nor will this soothe the sting of losing. Enough, you were distracted; and more than I.

SALADIN: Than you? What would have distracted *you*?

---

[26]The Imam was a leader of the Muslim community. The "smooth stones, which don't remind us of anything," are a reference to the Islamic prohibition on producing images or figures that might encourage idolatry.

SITTAH: Certainly not your distraction!—Oh Saladin, when will we play like this again?

SALADIN: We'll play harder than ever! Ah! Because it's starting again, you mean? Perhaps! Well, let it! I wasn't the one who drew the first sword. I would have happily extended the cease-fire again; would have happily found a good husband for my Sittah at the same time. And that would have been Richard's brother: yes, Richard's brother.[27]

SITTAH: How you love to praise your Richard!

SALADIN: If only our brother Melek had married Richard's sister.[28] Oh! What a house we'd have! Oh! The best house in the world, the best of the best! You know I'm not lazy about praising myself. I consider myself worthy of my friends. But *that* would have produced human beings!

SITTAH: Didn't I laugh at these beautiful dreams? You don't know the Christians, don't want to know them. Their pride is to be Christians, not human beings. For even those things that their Founder gave them, those things that season superstition with humanity, they don't love because they are humane, but because Christ taught them, because Christ did them. Lucky for them he was such a good person. Lucky for them they can take his virtue on trust and faith! But what virtue? Not his virtue. His name has to be spread everywhere, has to slander and swallow up the names of all good people. For them it's all about the name, only the name.

SALADIN: You mean: why they still demand that you and Melek be called Christians before you're allowed to love Christians?

SITTAH: Exactly! As though only Christians, as Christians, should be able to make use of the love that the Creator gave man and woman!

SALADIN: The Christians believe such pathetic things that they might as well believe this too! But still you're mistaken. It's the Templars, not the Christians, who are to blame. They're not to blame as Christians, but as Templars. Its because of them alone that nothing became of the plan. They simply don't want to give up Acre,[29]

---

[27]The reference is to Richard I (1157–1199), better known as Richard the Lion-Hearted, and his brother, Prince John (1167–1216), the future King John I of England. There is no historical evidence of a marriage plan for John and Sittah.

[28]Richard did propose a marriage alliance between his sister Joanna and Saladin's brother Melek and their joint rule over Jerusalem, but the Church rejected the plan.

[29]See note 22.

which Richard's sister was going to give our brother Melek as a dowry. To keep the knights' advantage they're playing the monk, the silly monk. And in case they might succeed in striking, they could hardly wait for the cease-fire to end. Funny! Keep it up, sirs, keep it up! Fine with me! If only everything else were as it should be.

SITTAH: Well? What else is bothering you? What else could have upset you?

SALADIN: What's always upset me. I've been to Lebanon, to see our father. He's still overwhelmed with worries.

SITTAH: Oh dear!

SALADIN: He can't make it. He's pinched everywhere. He's short here, short there.

SITTAH: Short of what? What's he missing?

SALADIN: What else but what I hardly think worth naming? The thing that, when I have it, seems so redundant, and when I don't have it, seems so indispensable. What's taking Al-Hafi so long? Is nobody looking for him? Confounded, cursed money! Thank goodness you're here, Hafi.

Scene 2

The Dervish Al-Hafi, Saladin, and Sittah.

AL-HAFI: I suppose the money from Egypt has arrived. Hopefully there's plenty of it.

SALADIN: Do you have any news?

AL-HAFI: Me? Not me. I thought I would get it here.

SALADIN: Give Sittah a thousand dinars. [*In his thoughts going back and forth.*]

AL-HAFI: Give! Instead of get! Oh great! That's even worse than getting nothing. To Sittah? To Sittah again? You've lost? You've lost at chess again? The game's still standing!

SITTAH: You'll grant me my good luck, won't you?

AL-HAFI: [*Looking at the game.*] Grant, what? When—you know well.

SITTAH: [*Waving at him.*] Sh! Hafi! Sh!

AL-HAFI: [*Still looking at the game.*] Grant it to yourself first!

SITTAH: Al-Hafi, sh!

AL-HAFI: [*To Sittah.*] You were white? You have him in check?

SITTAH: Good thing he can't hear us.

AL-HAFI: Now it's his move?

SITTAH: [*Coming closer to him.*] So do I get my money?

AL-HAFI: [*Still fixed on the game.*] Oh yes. You'll get it, just like you always do.

SITTAH: What? Are you mad?

AL-HAFI: The game isn't over. You haven't lost, Saladin.

SALADIN: [*Hardly listening.*] Well? Well? Pay! Pay!

AL-HAFI: Pay! Pay! There's your queen.

SALADIN: [*Still hardly listening.*] Doesn't count. Doesn't belong to the game anymore.

SITTAH: Just do it, and see to it that I can pick up my money.

AL-HAFI: [*Still absorbed in the game.*] Of course, just like always. Even so, even if the queen doesn't count, you're still not in mate.

SALADIN: [*Steps up and throws the game over.*] I am, I want to be.

AL-HAFI: Alright! The stakes are as legitimate as the game. They're both a farce!

SALADIN: [*To Sittah.*] What is he saying? What?

SITTAH: [*From time to time waving at Al-Hafi.*] You know him. He likes to be stubborn, likes to be asked. He must also be a little jealous.

SALADIN: But not of you. Of my sister? What do I hear, Hafi? Jealous? You?

AL-HAFI: Maybe! Maybe! I wish I had her brain, wish I were as good as she is.

SITTAH: Even so, he still hasn't paid me. And he'll pay me today. Just let him go! Just go, Al-Hafi, go! I want to be able to send for my money.

AL-HAFI: No. I can't play this game anymore. He has to know once and for all.

SALADIN: Who? And what?

SITTAH: Al-Hafi! Is this your promise? Is this how you keep your word?

AL-HAFI: How could I know it would go this far?

SALADIN: Well? Am I going to learn something?

SITTAH: I beg you, Al-Hafi. Be reasonable.

SALADIN: This is very strange! What could Sittah so solemnly, so cordially ask of a stranger, of a dervish, that she couldn't ask of me, her own brother. Al-Hafi, now I order you. Speak, dervish!

SITTAH: My brother, don't let a trifle come closer to you than it deserves to. You know, I've won the same amount from you in chess many times. And since I don't need the money now, and since the money in Al-Hafi's treasury isn't exactly piled up, the payments have been left where they are. But don't worry! I'm not going to give them to you, or Al-Hafi, or the treasury.

AL-HAFI: If it were only that! That!

SITTAH: And more of the same. What you once set aside for me has also stayed in the treasury for a few months.

AL-HAFI: Still not everything.

SALADIN: Not yet? Will you talk?

AL-HAFI: While we've been waiting for the money from Egypt, she's . . .

SITTAH: [*To Saladin.*] Why listen to him?

AL-HAFI: . . . not only taken nothing . . .

SALADIN: Good girl! And advances too, right?

AL-HAFI: She's kept the whole court going, fought your expenses all by herself.

SALADIN: Ha! That, that's my sister! [*hugging her*]

SITTAH: Who else could have made me rich enough to do this but you, my brother?

AL-HAFI: She'll soon make herself as poor as a beggar, just like her brother.

SALADIN: Me, poor? Her brother poor? When have I had more, when have I had less? One suit, one sword, one horse—and one God! What more do I need? When would I be lacking those? And yet, Al-Hafi, I could scold you.

SITTAH: Don't scold, my brother. If only I could ease the burdens of our father as well.

SALADIN: Oh! Oh! Now you've beaten my happiness down again! I'm not lacking anything, nor can I. But he's lacking, and therefore we're all lacking. Tell me, what should I do? There still might not be anything coming from Egypt for a long time. Why that is, God knows. Everything there is still calm. I'm happy to endure deprivation, reductions, saving when it only affects me, but only when it affects me and no one else. But what can that help? I must have one horse, one suit, one sword. And my God is also not negotiable. He's satisfied with so little. With my heart. But I had really counted on the surplus from your treasury, Hafi.

AL-HAFI: Surplus? Tell me yourself whether you wouldn't have had me impaled, or at least strangled, if I had been in possession of a surplus of yours. I'd rather risk embezzlement!

SALADIN: Well then, what should we do? Can't you borrow from anyone else but Sittah?

SITTAH: Would I have allowed this privilege to be taken from me, brother? And by him? Even now I insist on it. I'm not totally broke yet.

SALADIN: Only not totally! That takes the cake. Go immediately, make arrangements, Hafi. Take from whomever you can, and however you can! Go, borrow, promise. Only don't borrow from those whom I've made rich, Hafi. For borrowing from them would be the same thing as asking them to repay me. Go to the stingiest. They'll be happiest to lend to me. Since they know how well their money appreciates in my hands.

AL-HAFI: I don't know anyone like that.

SITTAH: It occurs to me, Hafi, that I've heard your friend is back.

AL-HAFI: [*Concerned.*] Friend? My friend? Who would that be?

SITTAH: Your highly praised Jew.

AL-HAFI: Praised Jew? Highly, from me?

SITTAH: To whom God—I think I remember correctly your having described him in this way—to whom his God gave, of all the goods in this world, the smallest and the greatest in full measure.

AL-HAFI: Did I say that? What did I mean by that?

SITTAH: The smallest: wealth. And the greatest: wisdom.

AL-HAFI: What? About a Jew? I said that about a Jew?

SITTAH: Didn't you say that about your Nathan?

AL-HAFI: Oh yes! About him! About Nathan! I hadn't thought about him. Really? He's finally come home? Oh! Then things might not be so bad with him after all. Right: his people have called him "the wise," and also "the rich."

SITTAH: They call him "the rich" more now than ever. The whole city's buzzing about the precious things, the treasures he brought back.

AL-HAFI: Well, then he's "the rich" again. So he must be "the wise" again too.

SITTAH: What if you were to approach him, Hafi?

AL-HAFI: And do what with him? Certainly not borrow? Don't you know him? Nathan, lend money? His wisdom is just that, that he doesn't lend to anyone.

SITTAH: In the past you've painted a very different picture of him.

AL-HAFI: If necessary he'll lend goods. But money, money? Never money. It's true he's the kind of Jew you don't see very often. He's reasonable. He knows how to live. He's a good chess player. But he's different from all other Jews in his bad features no less than in his good ones. Just don't count on him. He gives to the poor, and perhaps as much as Saladin. If not quite as much, at least just as gladly. But completely without distinction. Jew and Christian and Muslim and Parsi,[30] they're all the same to him.

SITTAH: And such a man . . .

SALADIN: How is it that I've never heard of this man?

SITTAH: He wouldn't lend to Saladin? Not to Saladin, who would only use the money for others, not himself?

AL-HAFI: Now you're only seeing the Jew again, the really common Jew! But believe me! He is so envious of your generosity, so envious! He'd like to keep every "may God reward you" that's said in the world for himself! It's only for that reason that he doesn't lend, so he always has something to give. Because his law commands charity but not compliance, charity makes him one of the most uncompliant people in the world. Of course, for some time I haven't been on such good terms with him. But don't think that for this reason I wouldn't give him his due. He's good for everything, but not for that. Just really not for that. Now I'm about to go. I'll knock on other doors. It occurs to me that I know a Moor[31] who is rich and stingy. I'm going, I'm going.

SITTAH: What's the hurry, Hafi?

SALADIN: Let him go! Let him go!

---

[30]Parsis were Zoroastrians, or adherents to the religion of the ancient Persian prophet Zoroaster (628–551 B.C.E.), who lived principally in and around Bombay, India.

[31]The term "Moor" (Ger: *Mohr*) was imprecise. Originally used to identify people from northwest Africa (e.g., Mauritania and Morocco), by Lessing's time it had come to refer also to black Africans, Muslim or otherwise.

Scene 3

Sittah and Saladin.

SITTAH: But he's hurrying as if he'd like to get away from me! What does that mean? Has he really been deceived, or—is he hoping to deceive us?

SALADIN: What? You're asking me? I hardly know whom you were speaking about; and just heard about your Jew, your Nathan, for the first time today.

SITTAH: Is it possible? That a man could stay so hidden from you, a man about whom it is said that he has explored Solomon's and David's tombs and knows how to loosen their seals with a powerful secret word?[32] From them, it is said, he occasionally brings to light such immeasurable treasures that no other source could produce.

SALADIN: If this man's riches came from tombs, they certainly weren't David's or Solomon's. Fools are buried there!

SITTAH: Or scoundrels! In any case his source of riches is far more abundant, far more inexhaustible than such a tomb filled with Mammon.[33]

SALADIN: Because he's a businessman, as I've heard.

SITTAH: His beasts of burden push through every street, pull through every desert. His ships lie in every harbor. Al-Hafi himself told me that already. And he was full of delight when he added how greatly, how nobly this friend of his made use of what he wasn't too proud to earn. And he added how free from prejudice his mind was, how open his heart was to every virtue, how harmonious it was with everything beautiful.

SALADIN: And yet Hafi just spoke so uncertainly, so coldly of him.

SITTAH: Not coldly, really. He was ill at ease, as though he considered it dangerous to praise him and yet didn't want to rebuke him undeservedly. Or could it really be that even the best of a people cannot completely escape his people, that for this reason Al-Hafi really had something to be ashamed of in his friend? Be that as it may! Whether the Jew is more or less the Jew, he's rich: that's enough for us!

---

[32]According to legend, Solomon had entombed his father, David, with a vast treasure, which could be summoned by a magic word.

[33]That is, wealth, lucre.

SALADIN: You don't want to take his wealth by force, do you, sister?

SITTAH: Well, what do you mean by force? With fire and sword? No, no, what force do you need against the weak but their own weakness? For now just come with me to my harem and listen to a singer I just bought yesterday. In the meantime a plan might ripen in my mind for this Nathan. Come!

Scene 4

Scene: In front of Nathan's house, adjacent to the palms.

Recha and Nathan come out. Daja comes toward them.

RECHA: You've lingered a long time, my father. I'm sure he's no longer there.

NATHAN: Now, now. If he's no longer here under the palms, he'll be somewhere else. Just stay calm now. Look! Isn't that Daja coming toward us?

RECHA: She's definitely lost track of him.

NATHAN: I don't think so.

RECHA: Otherwise she'd come more quickly.

NATHAN: But she hasn't seen us yet.

RECHA: Now she sees us.

NATHAN: And is walking twice as fast. See? Just stay calm! Calm!

RECHA: Would you really want a daughter who could be calm here? Who would let herself be unconcerned for the one whose good deed saved her life? Her life, which is only so dear, because she has you to thank for it?

NATHAN: I wouldn't want you any different than you are: even if I knew that something completely different was stirring in your soul.

RECHA: What, my father?

NATHAN: You're asking me? So timidly? Whatever is going on inside you is nature and innocence. Don't worry about it. Myself, I'm not worried. Only promise me: should your heart make itself more audibly clear, don't hide its wishes from me.

RECHA: Just the thought of my heart veiling itself from you makes me shudder.

NATHAN: No more of this! The matter is settled once and for all. Here comes Daja. Well?

DAJA: He's still wandering here under the palms, and will soon come around that wall. See, there he is!

RECHA: Ah! And seems undecided on where to go, whether further, or down, or right, or left.

DAJA: No, no. He's made his way around the monastery many times before, and has to come by here, don't you think?

RECHA: Right! Right! Have you spoken to him yet? And how is he today?

DAJA: As always.

NATHAN: Just see to it that he doesn't notice you here. Step back more. Better still, go all the way inside.

RECHA: Just one more look! Ah! The hedge that steals him from me.

DAJA: Come! Come! Father is quite right. You run the risk, if he sees you, that he'll turn around on the spot.

RECHA: Ah! The hedge!

NATHAN: And just as soon as he's stepped out from behind it, he won't be able to help seeing you. So just go!

DAJA: Come! Come! I know a window we can watch them from.

RECHA: Really? [*Both go inside.*]

Scene 5

Nathan and soon thereafter the Knight Templar.

NATHAN: This strange person almost frightens me. His raw virtue almost startles me. How one human being can make another so ill at ease! Ha! He's coming! By God! The youngster looks like a man. How I like his good, defiant look, his sturdy walk. The shell might be bitter; the core certainly isn't. But where have I seen someone like him before?—Excuse me, noble Frank . . .

TEMPLAR: What?

NATHAN: May I . . .

TEMPLAR: What, Jew? What?

NATHAN: . . . dare to speak to you.

TEMPLAR: Can I help it? Just make it quick.

NATHAN: Wait, and don't rush away so proudly, so contemptuously from a man to whom you have bound yourself forever.

TEMPLAR: What's that? Ah, I can almost guess. No? You're . . .

NATHAN: My name is Nathan. I'm the father of the girl your generosity saved from the fire, and have come . . .

TEMPLAR: If it's to thank me, save it! I've already had to endure far too much thanks for this trifle. And you owe me absolutely nothing. Did I know then that this girl was your daughter? It's the Templars' duty to jump to the aid of the first person they see in need. On top of that, at that moment my life was a burden to me. I was happy, very happy for the chance to risk it for another life: for another one—even if it was only the life of a Jewess.

NATHAN: Great! Great and horrible! But this turn of phrase is quite understandable. Modest greatness takes refuge behind the horrible to avoid admiration. But when it disdains the offer of admiration: then what kind of offering does it disdain less? Knight, if you weren't a foreigner and a prisoner, I wouldn't ask you so brazenly. Tell me, order me: how can I serve you?

TEMPLAR: You? With nothing.

NATHAN: I'm a rich man.

TEMPLAR: To me the rich Jew has never been the better Jew.

NATHAN: But despite that, wouldn't you prefer to make use of the better things he has? To make use of his wealth?

TEMPLAR: Fine then, I wouldn't deny that. For the sake of my cloak I wouldn't. As soon as it's completely worn out, when neither the stitches nor the cloth will hold any longer, I'll come and borrow from you, cloth or money, so I can get a new one. Now don't look so gloomy! You're still safe. It hasn't gotten that far yet. You see, it's still in pretty good shape. Only this one corner has a nasty stain. It's singed. And that happened when I carried your daughter through the fire.

NATHAN: [*Reaching for the corner and looking closely at it.*] But it's strange that such a bad stain, that such a brand could bear better witness than his own mouth. I could kiss it, that stain! Oh, pardon me! I didn't mean to do that.

TEMPLAR: What?

NATHAN: A tear fell on it.

TEMPLAR: It's nothing! It's seen plenty of drops. [*Aside:* This Jew is starting to confuse me.]

NATHAN: Would you be so good as to send your cloak just once to my girl?

TEMPLAR: What for?

NATHAN: So that her mouth could also press against this stain. Since the desire to embrace you around the knees has been in vain.

TEMPLAR: But, Jew—Your name is Nathan? But, Nathan—Your words are very—very good—very fine—I'm embarrassed—All the same—I would . . .

NATHAN: Pretend and feign all you like. I can see through you. You were too good, too decent to be polite. The girl, all feeling; the female envoy, all eagerness; the father far away. You took care of their reputations, fled their temptation; fled, in order not to conquer. For that too I thank you.

TEMPLAR: I have to confess, you know, how Templars are supposed to think.

NATHAN: Only Templars? Only "supposed to"? And just because the rules of the order command them to? I know how good human beings think; know that there are good human beings in all lands.

TEMPLAR: With differences, though, hopefully?

NATHAN: Certainly. Differences in color and clothing, in form.

TEMPLAR: And more or less depending on where you are.

NATHAN: These differences don't mean much. The great man needs a lot of room wherever he is. And when many of them are planted too closely together, they simply break each other's branches. But ordinary men like us always put up with crowds. Only the one mustn't carp at the others. The branch has to deal nicely with the swelling growths, and the treetop mustn't consider itself the only thing that came out of the ground.

TEMPLAR: Very well said! But you know the people that first started all this carping? Do you know, Nathan, which people first called itself the Chosen People? Well? And if I now don't hate these people but still can't help having contempt for them because of their pride? Their pride, which they left behind to the Christians and Muslims, in believing that only their God is the true God. You're startled that I, a Christian, a Templar, am talking this way? When and where has the frenzy of claiming possession of the better God, of forcing this better God upon the whole world for its own good, shown itself in a more dismal form than here and now? Who here and now hasn't had the scales fall from his eyes ... But be blind if you like! Forget what I said and leave me alone! [*Wants to go.*]

NATHAN: Ha! You don't know how much closer this makes me want to come to you. Come, we must, must be friends! Disdain my people as much as you like. Neither of us has chosen his people. Are we our people? What does "people" mean? Are Christians and Jews more Christians and Jews than human beings? Ah! Could it be that I've found in you another person for whom it's enough to be called a human being?

TEMPLAR: Yes, by God, you've found him, Nathan! You have! Your hand! I'm ashamed that I misjudged you for a moment.

NATHAN: And I'm proud of it. Only the common is rarely misjudged.

TEMPLAR: And rare things are hard to forget. Nathan, yes, we must, must become friends.

NATHAN: Are already. How happy my Recha will be! And ah! What a happy future is opening up before my eyes! Wait 'til you get to know her.

TEMPLAR: I'm burning with longing. Who's that running out of your house? Isn't it your Daja?

NATHAN: Absolutely. So fearful?

TEMPLAR: Has something happened to our Recha?

Scene 6

Daja, hurrying, and the previous.

DAJA: Nathan! Nathan!

NATHAN: Well?

DAJA: Pardon me, noble knight, for having to interrupt you.

NATHAN: Well, what is it?

TEMPLAR: What is it?

DAJA: The Sultan has sent a message. The Sultan wants to speak to you. God, the Sultan!

NATHAN: Me? The Sultan? He must be curious to see what new things I've brought back. Just say a little or nothing at all has been unpacked.

DAJA: No, no. He doesn't want to see anything, just wants to speak to you, you, in person, and soon, as soon as you can.

NATHAN: I'll come. Just go on, then, go!

DAJA: Beg your pardon, noble knight. God, we're so worried about what the Sultan wants.

NATHAN: We'll see soon enough. Go now, go!

Scene 7

Nathan and the Templar.

TEMPLAR: So you don't know him yet—I mean, personally?

NATHAN: Saladin? Not yet. I haven't avoided him, but also haven't tried to meet him. His general reputation was far too good for me not to prefer believing to seeing. But now, in this case, he has, by sparing your life . . .

TEMPLAR: Yes. It is definitely justified. The life I live is his gift.

NATHAN: From which he has doubly, triply given me life. This has changed everything between us. It has suddenly thrown a rope around me that will forever bind me in his service. I can hardly wait to see what he'll command me to do first. I'm ready for anything, and ready, thanks to you, to confess that I am.

TEMPLAR: I still haven't had the chance to thank him myself, though I've crossed his path so many times. The impression I made on him came so quickly, as quickly as it disappeared. Who knows if he even remembers me? And yet he must at least once remember me to decide my fate completely. It's not enough that I still exist by his order, that I'm still alive *thanks to* his will. Now I must wait for him to tell me according to *whose* will I have to live.

NATHAN: Exactly. All the more reason for me not to delay. There might be an occasion for me to bring that up during the conversation. Allow me, pardon me—I'm in a hurry—But when, when will we see you at our house?

TEMPLAR: As soon as I may.

NATHAN: As soon as you'd like.

TEMPLAR: Today.

NATHAN: And your name? I have to ask.

TEMPLAR: My name was—is—Curd von Stauffen. Curd!

NATHAN: Von Stauffen? Stauffen? Stauffen?

TEMPLAR: Why does that stand out for you?

NATHAN: Von Stauffen? There are many in that family . . .

TEMPLAR: Oh yes! Here there were, here many of the family lie rotting. My uncle himself—or my father, I should say—but why are you looking more and more sharply at me?

NATHAN: Oh nothing! Oh nothing! How could I tire of seeing you?

TEMPLAR: Then I'll leave you first. The curious person's look has often found more than it wished to find. I'm afraid of it, Nathan. Let time, not curiosity, gradually make our acquaintance. [*He leaves.*]

NATHAN: [*Watching him, astonished.*] "The curious person's look has often found more than it wished to find." It's as if he could read into my soul! Yes, truly. That could also happen to me. Not only Wolf's build, Wolf's walk: his voice too. Wolf even tossed his head just like that, absolutely just like that. Wolf even carried his sword just like that, and at the same time stroked his eyebrows with his hand to hide the fire of his gaze. How such deeply imprinted images can sometimes sleep within us, until a word, a sound awakens them. Von Stauffen! Quite right, quite right. Filnek and Stauffen. I want to know more soon, soon. But first to Saladin. But what's that? Isn't that Daja lurking there? Now just come closer, Daja.

Scene 8

Daja and Nathan.

NATHAN: Now I'm sure both of you are burning to learn something very different from what Saladin wants from me.

DAJA: Can you blame her? You just started speaking so intimately with him when the Sultan's message shooed us away from the window.

NATHAN: Well then, just tell her she can expect him any minute.

DAJA: Really? Really?

NATHAN: But can I really count on you, Daja? Be on your guard, I beg you. You won't regret it. And your conscience itself will tell you it's right. Just don't spoil anything in my plan. Just speak and ask modestly, with restraint.

DAJA: That you could still remember such a thing! I'm going. You go yourself. Look! I think a second messenger of the Sultan is coming, Al-Hafi, your dervish. [*Exit.*]

Scene 9

Nathan and Al-Hafi.

AL-HAFI: Hey! Hey! I was just about to come and see you.

NATHAN: Is it so urgent? What's he demanding of me?

AL-HAFI: Who?

NATHAN: Saladin. I'm coming, I'm coming.

AL-HAFI: To whom? To Saladin?

NATHAN: Didn't Saladin send you?

AL-HAFI: Me? No. Has he sent for you?

NATHAN: Yes, he certainly has.

AL-HAFI: Well, it's a good thing.

NATHAN: What? What's a good thing?

AL-HAFI: That . . . it's not my fault. God knows, it's not my fault. What I haven't said, what lies I haven't told, to prevent it!

NATHAN: To prevent what? What's a good thing?

AL-HAFI: That now you've become his defterdar. I feel sorry for you. But I don't want to witness it. I'm going now. I'm going. You've already heard where, and know the way. Tell me if you have anything to order from there. I'm at your service. Of course it can't be anything more than what a ragged man can carry. I'm going, so tell me soon.

NATHAN: Think about it, Al-Hafi. Think about the fact that I don't know anything about this. What are you chattering about?

AL-HAFI: You're bringing the purse with you right away?

NATHAN: Purse?

AL-HAFI: Well, the money that you're supposed to lend Saladin.

NATHAN: And there's nothing else?

AL-HAFI: I'm supposed to witness him hollow you out every day down to your toes? Supposed to watch while extravagance from the otherwise never empty barns of temperance borrows, and borrows, and borrows until the poor mice inside starve? Do you flatter yourself that the one who needs your money will also follow your advice? Right, imagine him following advice! When has Saladin ever let himself be advised? Just think, Nathan, what just now happened to me with him.

NATHAN: Well?

AL-HAFI: There I come to him, just after he's played chess with his sister. Sittah doesn't play too badly. And the game that Saladin thought was lost and had already given up is still standing there. And I see that the game is far from lost.

NATHAN: Wow! That was a great find for you!

AL-HAFI: He only had to protect his king with his pawn to get out of check. If only I could show you!

NATHAN: Oh, I trust you!

AL-HAFI: Because then his rook would have been free to move, and she would have been done for. And I want to show him all this and call him. Imagine!

NATHAN: He disagrees with you?

AL-HAFI: He doesn't even listen to me, and contemptuously throws the whole game into a heap.

NATHAN: Is that possible?

AL-HAFI: And says he wants to be in mate once and for all. He wants to be! Is that playing?

NATHAN: Hardly, more like playing with playing.

AL-HAFI: All the same it didn't count for anything.

NATHAN: Never mind the money! That's the least of it. But not even listening to you! Not even listening to you about a point of such importance! Not admiring your eagle eye! That, that calls for revenge, doesn't it?

AL-HAFI: Oh, never mind. I tell you this only so you can see what kind of head he has. In short, I, I can't stand being with him anymore. So now I have to run to every dirty Moor and ask who wants to lend to him. I, who have never begged for myself, am now supposed to borrow for others. Borrowing isn't much better than begging, just as lending, lending at usury, isn't much better than stealing. Among my Guebres[34] on the Ganges I don't need either one, and don't need to be the tool of either one. On the Ganges, only on the Ganges are there human beings. Here you're the only

---

[34]Guebres were Zoroastrians. See note 30. The unlikely fact of a dervish, that is, a Muslim, referring to Guebres or Zoroastrians as "his" can be attributed either to Lessing's confusion over the different religions or to a deliberate attempt on his part to show the malleability and compatibility of differing religious traditions.

one who deserves to live on the Ganges. Will you come with me? Leave him in the lurch with his plunder once and for all. He's going to take it from you bit by bit anyway. This way you can end the unpleasant job at once. I'll get you a Delk.[35] Come! Come!

NATHAN: I would think we could always do that. But, Al-Hafi, I'll think it over. Wait . . .

AL-HAFI: Think it over? No, something like this you don't think over.

NATHAN: Just 'til I come back from the Sultan, 'til I take leave . . .

AL-HAFI: Whoever thinks it over is looking for reasons not to be able to do it. Whoever can't decide on a moment's notice to live for himself will be a slave to others forever. As you like it! Farewell! As you please. My way is there, yours is here.

NATHAN: Al-Hafi! You don't even want to settle your accounts?

AL-HAFI: What a joke! The holdings in my bank aren't worth counting. And you or Sittah can vouch for my debts. Farewell! [*Exit.*]

NATHAN: [*Watching him.*] I'll vouch for it! Wild, good, noble, what should I call him? The true beggar is the one and only true king! [*Exit from another side.*]

ACT 3

Scene 1

Scene: In Nathan's house.

Recha and Daja.

RECHA: Daja, how did my father express himself? "I can expect him at any moment"? That sounds—doesn't it—as though he would appear so soon. But how many moments have already passed! Oh well: who thinks about the past? I only want to live in each new moment. And the one that brings him will eventually come.

DAJA: Oh, that cursed message from the Sultan! Without it Nathan would have brought him here right away.

RECHA: And if he came now, at this moment, if my warmest, most heartfelt wishes were fulfilled, then what? Then what?

---

[35] In a letter to his brother Karl, Lessing wrote that a Delk was "in Arabic the name of a dervish's smock." Karl Lachmann and Franz Muncker, eds., *Gotthold Ephraim Lessings sämtliche Schriften,* vol. 18 (Leipzig, 1907), 313.

DAJA: Then what? Then I hope that my warmest wishes would also be fulfilled.

RECHA: What will then take its place in my chest, which without a ruling wish of wishes, has forgotten how to swell? Nothing? Oh, I'm afraid!

DAJA: My wish, mine will then take its place. Mine. My wish to see you in Europe, to know you are in hands that are worthy of you.

RECHA: You're wrong. What makes this wish yours is exactly what prevents it from ever becoming mine. You're drawn to your people. And mine? Mine shouldn't keep me? An image of your people that hasn't dissolved in your soul should be worth more than the one I can see, and touch, and hear—my people?

DAJA: Resist all you want! The ways of heaven are the ways of heaven. And if your savior himself, through whom his God, for whom he fights, should wish to lead you into the land and to the people for which you were born?

RECHA: Daja! There you go again, dear Daja! You really have peculiar ideas! "His, his God! for whom he fights!" Who owns God? What kind of God is it that human beings could own, that has to be fought for by human beings? And how do you know what clod of earth you're born *for* if it's not for the one that you were born *on*? If only my father heard you like this! What did he do to you to make you always pretend that my happiness is as far away from him as possible? What did he do to you to make you so happy to mix the seeds of reason, which he sowed so purely in my soul, with the weeds or flowers of your land? Dear, dear Daja, he doesn't want your colorful flowers on my soil! And I have to say to you, when they cover my soil it strikes me as sapped, ravaged by your flowers. To me their scents are bittersweet; they make me so numb, so dizzy! Your brain is more used to them. I don't blame you for having strong enough nerves to handle them. It's just that they're not my taste. And your angel, how close did he come to making a fool out of me? I'm still ashamed to look at my father after that farce!

DAJA: Farce! As if reason were only at home here! Farce! Farce! If only I could speak!

RECHA: Can't you? When wasn't I all ears, whenever you felt like entertaining me with your stories about the heroes of the faith? Haven't I always been happy to show my admiration for their deeds and to cry over their sufferings? It's true that their faith never

seemed to me to be their most heroic feature. I found more com-
forting their teaching that submission to God is entirely independent of our speculations about God. Dear Daja, my father has said
that so many times and you yourself have agreed with him so often
on that point. Why are you destroying by yourself what you built
together with him? Dear Daja, this isn't the kind of conversation we
should greet our friend with. Of course, it's fine with me, since the
most important thing for me is to know if he . . . Listen, Daja! Isn't
someone coming to our door? I hope it's him! Listen!

Scene 2

*Recha, Daja, and the Templar, for whom someone outside is holding the
door and saying:*

Go inside here!

RECHA: [*Nearly collides with the Templar, pulls herself together, and is
about to fall to his feet.*]

TEMPLAR: I came late simply to avoid this. And yet—

RECHA: I only want to thank God at the feet of this proud man. I don't
want to thank the man. He doesn't want any thanks. He wants it as
little as the water bucket that proved to be so useful at dousing. It
let itself be filled, let itself be emptied, nothing to me, nothing to
you. The man is the same way. He too was only shoved into the
fire. Then I happened to fall into his arms. There I happened to
stay, like a spark on his cloak, in his arms. Until something, I don't
know what, shoved us both out of the fire. What's there to thank?
In Europe wine drives people to much greater deeds. Templars,
they just have to behave this way. They have to be somewhat better
trained dogs to fetch from the fire as well as the water.

TEMPLAR: [*Looking at her with astonishment and uneasiness.*] Oh Daja,
Daja! If in moments of worry and anger my mood was rude to you,
why bring every foolishness that seized my tongue back to her?
Your vengeance was too cruel, Daja! If you'd please represent me to
her more fairly from now on.

DAJA: I don't think, knight, I don't think these little barbs that she
threw at your heart have hurt you much.

RECHA: What? You had worries? And were stingier with your worries
than with your life?

TEMPLAR: Good, sweet child! How my soul is divided between eye and ear. This wasn't the girl, no, no, this wasn't the girl I pulled out of the fire. For who could have known her and not pulled her out of the fire? Who would have waited for me? Yet—fear—distorts. [*Pause during which he seems to lose himself in contemplation of her.*]

RECHA: But I find you the same as you were. [*Another pause; until she continues, trying to interrupt his staring.*] Now, knight, tell us then where you've been so long? I could almost ask: where are you now?

TEMPLAR: I am—where maybe I shouldn't be.

RECHA: Where you were? Also maybe where you shouldn't have been? That's not good.

TEMPLAR: On—on—what's the mountain called? On Mount Sinai.

RECHA: On Mount Sinai? How nice! Now I can finally learn for sure whether it's true . . .

TEMPLAR: What? What? Whether it's true that you can still see the place where Moses stood before God when . . .

RECHA: No, no, not that. Wherever he stood, he was standing before God. And I'm familiar enough with all that. I'd like to learn from you whether it isn't nearly as hard to climb up this mountain as down. You see, every time I've climbed a mountain it's been the opposite. Well, knight? What? You're turning away from me? Don't want to see me?

TEMPLAR: Because I want to hear you.

RECHA: Because you don't want to show me that you're smiling at my simplemindedness? That you're smiling at how I couldn't ask anything more important about this holiest of all mountains? Isn't that right?

TEMPLAR: Still I have to look you in the eye again. What? Now you're casting your eyes down? Now you're holding back your smile at how I first want to read in facial expressions, in doubtful facial expressions, what I hear so clearly, what you say so distinctly. You're holding it back? Ah Recha! Recha! How right he was when he said, "Get to know her first!"

RECHA: Who said that to you? And about whom?

TEMPLAR: "Get to know her first!" Your father said that to me, about you.

DAJA: And didn't I say the same thing? Didn't I?

TEMPLAR: Only where is he? Where is your father? Is he still at the Sultan's?

RECHA: Without a doubt.

TEMPLAR: Still, still there? Oh, I'm so forgetful! No, no; he couldn't be there anymore. He's probably waiting for me down there by the monastery. Definitely. I mean, that was what we planned. Excuse me! I'm going, I'll get him . . .

DAJA: That's my job. Stay, knight, stay. I'll bring him right away.

TEMPLAR: Not like that, not like that! He's expecting me, not you. Besides, he could easily . . . who knows? With the Sultan he could easily . . . You don't know the Sultan! . . . easily get into difficulties. Believe me, there could be danger if I don't go.

RECHA: Danger? What kind of danger?

TEMPLAR: Danger for me, for you, for him: if I don't go quickly, quickly. [*Exit.*]

Scene 3

Recha and Daja.

RECHA: What's this, Daja? So quickly? What's the matter with him? What struck him? What's stalking him?

DAJA: Just leave him alone. I think it's not a bad sign.

RECHA: Sign? Of what?

DAJA: That something's happening inside. It's boiling, and shouldn't boil over. Just leave him alone. Now it's up to you.

RECHA: What's up to me? You're becoming, like him, incomprehensible to me.

DAJA: Soon you'll be able to pay him back for all the trouble he's caused you. But don't be all too severe, don't be all too vengeful.

RECHA: What you're talking about only you know.

DAJA: You're so calm again all of a sudden?

RECHA: I am, yes I am . . .

DAJA: At least admit that his uneasiness makes you happy, that it's thanks to his uneasiness that you feel at ease.

RECHA: I'm completely unaware of this! The most I could admit to you would be that it's strange to me how such calm could suddenly follow such a storm in my heart. His full appearance, his speech, his tone . . .

DAJA: Sated you?

RECHA: I wouldn't say sated me. No, hardly—

DAJA: Only stilled your hunger pangs.

RECHA: Well yes, if you like.

DAJA: Well I don't.

RECHA: He will always be dear to me, he'll stay dearer to me than my life, even if my pulse doesn't quicken at the sound of his name, even if my heart doesn't beat faster, harder whenever I think of him. What nonsense I'm talking! Come, come dear Daja, back to the window that overlooks the palms.

DAJA: Then they aren't completely stilled yet, your hunger pangs.

RECHA: Now I'll also see the palms again, not just him beneath the palms.

DAJA: This chill is only the beginning of a new fever.

RECHA: What chill? I'm not cold. I really don't see with less pleasure what I see with calm.

Scene 4

Scene: A reception hall in Saladin's palace.

Saladin and Sittah.

SALADIN: [*Walking in, toward the doors.*] Bring the Jew here as soon as he comes. He doesn't seem to be in too much of a hurry.

SITTAH: He wasn't exactly at hand, wasn't easy to find.

SALADIN: Sister! Sister!

SITTAH: You act as though you were about to go into battle.

SALADIN: And with weapons that I haven't learned to use. I'm supposed to dissimulate, to incite fear; supposed to lay traps, trick him. When have I ever been able to do that? Where would I have learned it? And why do I have to do all this? What for? To fish for money. Money! To scare up money, money from a Jew. Money! Have I finally been brought to such petty tricks, to get myself the most trifling of trifles?

SITTAH: Every trifle you scorn too much will avenge itself, brother.

SALADIN: All too true. And if this Jew is the good, reasonable man that the dervish described earlier?

SITTAH: Well then! Why would it be necessary? The snare lies only for the stingy, anxious, fearful Jew; not for the good, not for the wise man. This one is already ours, without a snare. The pleasure of hearing how such a man tries to talk his way out of it, with what daring strength he just rips through the cord, or with what sly caution he avoids the net: this pleasure you'll have anyway.

SALADIN: Well, that's true. I'm certainly looking forward to it.

SITTAH: Then nothing else can embarrass you. If he's just one of the crowd, if he's just a Jew like any other, then in front of him will you be ashamed to be what he thinks all people are? Even more, whoever shows himself better, to the Jew he's just an ass, a fool.

SALADIN: Then I have to act badly so the bad one doesn't think badly of me?

SITTAH: Really! If you call it acting badly to use such a thing after its own fashion.

SALADIN: What couldn't a woman's head invent that it couldn't put in a favorable light!

SITTAH: Put in a favorable light!

SALADIN: I'm just worried that this fine, sharp thing will break in my clumsy hand! Such a thing needs to be carried out as it was invented: with all cunning and agility. Be that as it may! I'll dance as well as I can, though I'd naturally rather do it well than badly.

SITTAH: Just don't trust yourself too little! I'll vouch for you if you don't! If only you want me to. How men such as you like to convince us that only their sword, their sword alone has brought them so far. The lion is naturally ashamed when it hunts with the fox— ashamed of the fox, not the cunning.

SALADIN: And how women like to bring men down to their level! Just go, go! I think I know my lesson.

SITTAH: What? I'm supposed to go?

SALADIN: You didn't want to stay, did you?

SITTAH: If not stay . . . in your sight, just here in the next room.

SALADIN: To listen? Not that either, sister, if you don't mind my insisting on it. Go! Go! The curtain is moving. He's coming! Don't stay there! I'll make sure. [*As she moves away from one door, Nathan steps in through the other; and Saladin has sat down.*]

Scene 5

Saladin and Nathan.

SALADIN: Step closer, Jew! Closer! All the way! But without fear!

NATHAN: Fear is for your enemies!

SALADIN: You call yourself Nathan?

NATHAN: Yes.

SALADIN: Wise Nathan?

NATHAN: No.

SALADIN: Right! You don't call yourself that. The people call you that.

NATHAN: Maybe; the people!

SALADIN: You don't think I have contempt for the voice of the people, do you? I've long wanted to meet a man they call "the wise."

NATHAN: And if they call him that to make fun of him? If to the people wise is nothing more than smart? And if only the one who understands what's in his interest is considered smart?

SALADIN: In his true interest, you mean?

NATHAN: Then the most selfish person would naturally be the smartest. Then smart and wise would naturally be the same thing.

SALADIN: I can hear you prove what you want to refute. You know the true interests of the people, which they themselves don't know. At least you've tried to find out, you've thought about them: this alone makes one wise.

NATHAN: As everyone considers himself to be.

SALADIN: Enough modesty! To keep hearing it when you expect dry reason is sickening. [*He jumps up.*] Let's get to the point! But, but honestly, Jew, honestly!

NATHAN: Sultan, I certainly want to serve you in such a way that I remain worthy of your business in the future.

SALADIN: Serve? What?

NATHAN: You should have the best of everything, and at the lowest of prices.

SALADIN: What are you talking about? Not your goods? Though my sister will be happy to haggle with you. [*Aside:* That's for the little eavesdropper!] I have nothing to do with businessmen.

NATHAN: Then you must want to know what I noticed or encountered on my trip about the enemy, who is of course stirring again? If I may be frank . . .

SALADIN: That's not where I'm headed with you either. I know as much about that as I need to. In brief . . .

NATHAN: Command, Sultan.

SALADIN: I request your instruction in something completely different, something completely different. Since you're so wise, then tell me: Which religion, which law makes the most sense to you?

NATHAN: Sultan, I'm a Jew.

SALADIN: And I'm a Muslim. The Christian is between us. Only one of these religions can be the true one. A man like you doesn't stay where the accident of birth threw him. Or when he does stay there, it's because of insight, reasons, the better choice. Now then! Share your insight with me. Let me hear the reasons that I haven't had the time to ponder. Let me know the choice—in confidence, naturally—that these reasons have determined, so I can make it mine. What? You're surprised? You're looking at me, trying to figure me out? It may very well be that I'm the first Sultan to have such a whim, which after all I don't think is so unworthy of a Sultan. Don't you agree? Then talk! Speak! Or do you want a moment to think it over? Fine, I'll give it to you. [*Aside:* I wonder if she's listening. Now I want to listen to her, to hear if I've done it right.] Think about it. Think about it quickly! I won't hesitate to come back. [*He goes into the next room, where Sittah has gone.*]

Scene 6

Nathan, alone.

Hm! Hm! Strange! What should I think? What does the Sultan want? What? I'm prepared for money, and he wants . . . truth. Truth! And he wants it like that, so bare, so shiny, as though the truth were a coin! Now if it were an ancient coin being weighed, that would be one thing. But such a new coin, that only a stamp can make, that you can just count on a counter, that's not what the truth is. Like money in a bag, can you rake truth into your head? Who's the Jew here? Me or him? But wait! What if in truth he's not asking for truth? Of course it would be too small to suspect him of using the truth as a trap! Too small? What's too small for a great man? Really, really, the way he blurted it out! You have to be gentler when you approach someone as a friend. I have to move carefully! But how? How should I? To be so completely Jewish won't work. And not to be Jewish at all will be worse. Since if I'm not Jewish, he could ask me, why not be a Muslim? That's it! That can save me! It's not just children who can be humored with fairy tales. He's coming. Let him come!

Scene 7

Saladin and Nathan.

SALADIN: [*Aside:* The coast is clear!] Am I coming back too soon? You're at the end of your reflections. Then talk! Not a soul can hear us.

NATHAN: Let the whole world hear us.

SALADIN: So sure Nathan is about the matter? Well! That's what I call a wise man! Never hiding the truth! Risking everything for it! Life and limb! His possessions and his blood!

NATHAN: Yes! Yes! When it's necessary and useful.

SALADIN: From now on I can hope to have rightfully as one of my titles, Improver of the World and of the Law.

NATHAN: Surely a lovely title! But, Sultan, before I tell you everything, may I tell you a story?

SALADIN: Why not? I've always been fond of well-told stories.

NATHAN: Now, telling stories *well* isn't exactly my talent.

SALADIN: So proudly modest again? Do it! Tell, tell!

NATHAN: Many years ago in the east there lived a man who owned a ring of inestimable worth, which someone dear to him had given him. The stone was an opal that sparkled with a hundred beautiful colors and had the mysterious power of making whoever wore it agreeable to God and human beings, as long as the wearer believed in its power. Is it any wonder that the man in the east never let it off his finger, or that he ordered it never to leave the possession of his family? And this is how it went. He left the ring to his favorite son, and stipulated that this son also leave the ring to the son he loved best. And always the favorite, owing only to his possession of the ring and without respect to his birth order, would be the head, the prince of the house. You understand me, Sultan?

SALADIN: I understand you. Go on!

NATHAN: The ring went in this way from son to son until it came to a father of three sons, all of whom were equally obedient and all of whom he therefore couldn't help loving equally. Yet from time to time the first one, or the second, or the third—at the moment when he found himself alone with one of them and the other two couldn't share the outpourings of his heart—seemed more worthy of the ring, and in his gentle weakness he promised it to each of them. This worked well enough for as long as it worked. But then it came time to die and the good father found himself in a difficult position. It grieved him to hurt in this way two of his sons, who trusted him in his word. What to do? He secretly sent for an artist and ordered, according to the design of his ring, two new ones, and he told him to spare no expense at making each of them identical, completely identical to his ring. The artist succeeded. When he brought the rings, the father himself couldn't tell which was the original. Happily and cheerfully he called for his sons, one at a time, and gave each one his special blessing, and his ring, then he died. Are you listening, Sultan?

SALADIN: [*Upset, turning away from him.*] I'm listening, I'm listening! Just finish your story quickly, will you?

NATHAN: I'm finished. What follows goes without saying. The father was hardly dead when each son came with his ring, and each wanted to be prince of the house. They scrutinized, bickered, complained. In vain. The true ring was indistinguishable—[*After a pause to wait for the Sultan's response.*]—almost as indistinguishable as the true religion is to us.

SALADIN: What? This is the answer to my question? . . .

NATHAN: Excuse me if I don't dare to distinguish between the rings that the father deliberately had made so that they couldn't be distinguished.

SALADIN: The rings! Don't play with me! I would have thought that the religions I mentioned were, on the contrary, quite easily distinguished. All the way down to their clothing, all the way down to their food and drink.

NATHAN: Just not in their foundations. After all, aren't they all grounded in history? Written or passed down! And history can only be accepted on faith and belief, right? Well, whose faith and belief are we least likely to call into question? Isn't it our own, that of the people to whom we belong? Of the people who from childhood on have given us proof of their love? Who never deceived us, except when deception was better for us? How can I believe my forefathers less than you believe yours, or vice versa? Can I demand that you charge your ancestors with lying, so that you don't contradict mine? Or vice versa? The same applies to the Christians, right?

SALADIN: [*Aside:* By God! The man is right. I should be quiet.]

NATHAN: Let's get back to our rings. As I was saying: the sons sued each other, and each swore to the judge that he had gotten the ring directly from his father's hand — And how true! — long after he had gotten the promise that he would one day enjoy the ring's privilege. No less true! Each asserted that his father could never have deceived him. And before suspecting such a dear father of this, each said, he was compelled to accuse his brothers of fraud — however ready he normally was to believe the best about them. And each said he wanted to find out who the traitor was, so he could avenge himself.

SALADIN: And then, the judge? I can't wait to hear what you'll have the judge say. Speak!

NATHAN: The judge said, "If you can't bring your father right here, then I order you away from my bench. Do you think I'm here to solve riddles? Or are you waiting for the true ring to open its mouth? But wait! I hear that the true ring has the miraculous power of making its wearer loved, agreeable to God and human beings. That should decide the matter! For the false rings couldn't do that! Well, which one of you do the other two love the most? Go ahead, say it! You're not saying anything? The rings only work in reverse, inwardly and not outwardly? Each of you loves himself the most? Oh, then all three of you are deceived deceivers! None of your rings is the real one. The real ring must have been lost. To hide the loss, to replace it, your father had three made for one."

SALADIN: Wonderful! Wonderful!

NATHAN: "And so," the judge continued, "if you'd rather have my ruling than my advice, then just leave. But my advice is that you take the case purely as it stands. Each of you has his ring from his father, so let each believe that he has the true one. But it's possible that your father could no longer stand the tyranny of *one* ring in his house! And it's certain that he loved all three of you, and equally, since he couldn't treat two of you unfairly to please the third. Let each of you rival the others only in uncorrupted love, free from prejudice. Let each of you strive to show the power of his ring's stone. Come to the aid of this power in gentleness, with heartfelt tolerance, in charity, with sincerest submission to God. And should the powers of the stone express themselves in your children's children's children, then let them come again before this bench. Then a wiser man than I will sit before them and rule. Go!" Thus spoke the modest judge.

SALADIN: God! God!

NATHAN: Saladin, if you feel you're this foretold wiser man . . .

SALADIN: [*Rushing toward him and gripping his hand, not letting it go.*] This dust? This nothing? O God!

NATHAN: What's the matter, Sultan?

SALADIN: Nathan, dear Nathan! Your judge's thousand years aren't over yet. His judge's bench isn't mine. Go! Go! But be my friend.

NATHAN: And Saladin has nothing more to say?

SALADIN: Nothing.

NATHAN: Nothing?

SALADIN: Nothing at all. Why?

NATHAN: I would have liked the opportunity to ask a favor of you.

SALADIN: Does asking a favor require an opportunity? Speak!

NATHAN: I've come back from a long trip, during which I collected debts. I almost have too much cash. The times are becoming worrisome again, and I don't know very well where it would be safe. So I wondered whether you might not need some, as coming war always needs money.

SALADIN: [*Looking him straight in the eye.*] Nathan! I won't ask whether Al-Hafi has been to see you, won't investigate whether some other suspicion has driven you to make this voluntary offer . . .

NATHAN: A suspicion?

SALADIN: I'm worthy of it. Forgive me! What's the use? I must admit to you that I had the idea . . .

NATHAN: Not of asking me for that?

SALADIN: It's true.

NATHAN: That would have helped both of us! If I can't send you all my money, that's because of the young Templar. Of course you know him. First I have to give him a large payment.

SALADIN: Templar? You wouldn't want to support my worst enemy with your money, would you?

NATHAN: I'm only speaking of the one whose life you spared.

SALADIN: Ah! What you've reminded me of! I'd completely forgotten this young man! Do you know him? Where is he?

NATHAN: What? Then you don't know how your grace toward him has flowed from him to me? He, risking his own newly spared life, he saved my daughter from a fire.

SALADIN: He did? He did that? Ha! He looked like that. My brother, whom he so resembles, would certainly have done the same thing! Is he still here? Then bring him to me! I've told my sister so much about this brother of hers whom she never met that I should let her see his spitting image! Go get him! How from *one* good deed, though born of pure feeling, so many other good deeds flow! Go get him!

NATHAN: [*Letting go of Saladin's hand.*] Right away! And we still have an agreement about the other thing? [*Exit.*]

SALADIN: Ah! If only I'd let my sister listen! I have to go to her! How can I tell her everything I've learned? [*Exit from the other side.*]

Scene 8

Scene: Beneath the palms near the monastery, where the Templar waits for Nathan.

TEMPLAR: [*Walking back and forth, struggling with himself, until he bursts forth.*] Here the tired sacrificial victim pauses. Alright! I can't know, can't know any better what's happening inside me. I can't fig- ure out what's going to happen. Suffice it to say I ran away in vain! In vain. And yet I couldn't do anything but run away! Now come what may! The blow fell too quickly to avoid it. I refused long and hard to come under it. Seeing her, whom I had so little desire to see — seeing her, and then the decision never to let her out of my sight. What decision? A decision is an intention, a deed. But I, I endured, I only endured. Seeing her, and the feeling of being bound up with her, of being interwoven with her, were one and the same. Remain one and the same. To live apart from her is completely unthinkable to me. That would be my death, and wherever I might go after death, it would be my death there too. If that's love, then the Templar truly loves, the Christian truly loves the Jewish girl. Hm! And so what? I've given up more than one prejudice in this praised land, and for that reason it will always be praised by me.[36] What does my order want? As a Templar I'm dead, was dead from the moment I became Saladin's prisoner. The head that Saladin granted me, was it my old one? It's a new one that doesn't know anything about what was talked into the old one and constrained it. And it's a better one, better suited to my father's Heaven. I truly feel that. For the first time I'm beginning to think as my father must have thought when he was here, if I haven't been deceived by fairy tales about him. Fairy tales? But very believable ones. They've never seemed more believable to me than now that I run the danger of stumbling where he fell. He fell? I would rather fall with men than stand with children. His example guarantees me his approval. And whose approval do I need besides his? Nathan's? From him I'll have encouragement, not only approval. What a Jew! And one who wants to be seen only as a Jew! Here he comes, he's hurrying, glowing with clear joy. But who ever came from Saladin not looking that way? Hey, hey Nathan!

Scene 9

Nathan and the Templar.

NATHAN: What? Is it you?

TEMPLAR: You stayed a long time at the Sultan's.

NATHAN: Not that long. I hesitated too long on the way there. Oh really, Curd, that man lives up to his reputation. His reputation is just his shadow. But before anything else let me quickly tell you . . .

TEMPLAR: What?

NATHAN: He wants to speak to you, wants you to come to him immediately. Just come back to my house, where I have something else for him, and then we'll go.

[36]This pun is untranslatable. In German "gelobtes Land" is equivalent to "Promised Land," though it literally means "praised land."

TEMPLAR: Nathan, I'd rather not go to your house . . .

NATHAN: But haven't you already been there? Haven't you already spoken to her? Well? Tell me, how do you like Recha?

TEMPLAR: Indescribably! But, to see her again, I'll never be able to do that! Never! Never! Unless you promise me right now that I'll be able to see her again and again, forever.

NATHAN: How am I supposed to understand that?

TEMPLAR: [*After a short pause throwing his arms around him.*] My father!

NATHAN: Young man!

TEMPLAR: [*Quickly letting go of him.*] Not "son"? I beg you, Nathan!

NATHAN: Dear young man!

TEMPLAR: Not "son"? I beg you, Nathan! I implore you, by the first bonds of nature! Don't prefer the chains that came later! Be content to be a human being. Don't push me away from you!

NATHAN: Dear, dear friend! . . .

TEMPLAR: And "son"? Not "son"? Not even if gratitude opened the way for love to reach your daughter's heart? Not even if both of us were just waiting for a sign from you to melt into one? You're not saying anything?

NATHAN: You surprise me, young knight.

TEMPLAR: I surprise you? Surprise you, Nathan, with your own thoughts? You're not disavowing them when they come out of my mouth, are you? I surprise you?

NATHAN: First I have to know which Stauffen your father was!

TEMPLAR: What are you saying, Nathan? What? At this moment nothing else occurs to you but curiosity?

NATHAN: But you see, I once knew a Stauffen named Conrad.

TEMPLAR: Well, what if that was my father's name?

NATHAN: Really?

TEMPLAR: I'm named after him. Curd is Conrad.

NATHAN: Well, then the Conrad I knew couldn't have been your father, since my Conrad was, like you, a Templar, was never married.

TEMPLAR: Oh, for that reason!

NATHAN: Well?

TEMPLAR: Despite that, he still could have been my father.

NATHAN: You're joking.

TEMPLAR: And you're taking my father's celibacy all too literally. What difference does it make? So what if I'm a bastard? We're not such a contemptible breed. Just spare me this probe into my ancestry, and I won't look into yours. Not that I have the slightest doubt about your family tree. God forbid! You could cover it leaf by leaf all the way back to Abraham. And from there even further, I know it myself. I'll testify to it myself.

NATHAN: You're becoming bitter. But do I deserve this? Have I refused you anything? It's just that at the moment I don't want to take you at your word. That's all.

TEMPLAR: Really? Nothing more? Oh, then forgive me!

NATHAN: Just come now, come!

TEMPLAR: Where? No! Home with you? Not that! Not that! There's fire there! I'll wait for you here. Go! If I see her again, I'll see her often enough. If not, then I've seen her far too much . . .

NATHAN: I'll go as quickly as I can.

Scene 10

The Templar and Daja following soon thereafter.

TEMPLAR: That's more than enough! The human brain can hold an unlimited amount, and then in one moment it's suddenly full! Suddenly a trifle fills it completely! Never mind, never mind. Let it be full of whatever it likes. Just be patient! Soon the soul will push the puffed-up thoughts together to make room for them, and light and order will come again. Am I in love for the first time? Or is what I thought love was not love? Is love what I feel now?

DAJA: [*Sneaking in from the side.*] Knight! Knight!

TEMPLAR: Who's that? Oh, Daja, is that you?

DAJA: I tried to sneak by him, but he could still see us where you're standing. So come closer to me, behind this tree.

TEMPLAR: What is it? Why so secretive? What is it?

DAJA: It *is* a secret that brings me to you, in fact a double secret. The first only I know, and the second only you know. What do you say we trade? Entrust me with yours, and I'll entrust you with mine.

TEMPLAR: With pleasure, as soon as I know what you think mine is. But that will be clear from yours. Just go ahead and start.

DAJA: But think! No, Sir knight. First you, then I'll follow. Since my secret can't help you at all if I don't already know yours. Now quickly! I've asked you first, so I haven't given anything away. My secret remains my secret, and you've already given yours away. Poor knight! Imagine you men being able to keep such a secret from us women!

TEMPLAR: Often we ourselves don't know we have one to keep.

DAJA: That may be. For that reason I have to be kind enough to acquaint you with yours. Say, what was the meaning of your running off without warning, leaving us in the lurch? Not coming home with Nathan? Has Recha had so little effect on you? Well? Or rather too much? So much! So much! You think you can teach me about the fluttering of the bird stuck to the snare! In short, just admit that you love her, that you love her to the point of madness, and I'll tell you what . . .

TEMPLAR: To the point of madness? That's something you should know a lot about.

DAJA: Just admit the part about love. We'll forget about the madness.

TEMPLAR: Because it goes without saying? A Templar in love with a Jewish girl!

DAJA: It's true, there doesn't seem to be much sense in that. But now and then there's more sense in something than we assume; and it wouldn't be so unheard of if the Savior led us onto paths that even the clever wouldn't easily walk.

TEMPLAR: So solemn? [*Aside:* And if I replaced the Savior with Providence, wouldn't she be right?] You're making me more curious than I'm used to being.

DAJA: Oh, this is the land of miracles!

TEMPLAR: [*Aside:* Well! Of miracles. Could it be otherwise? The whole world has crowded together here.] Dear Daja, supposing I told you what you're demanding: that I love her, that I don't know how I could live without her, that . . .

DAJA: Is it true? Is it true? Then swear to me, Sir knight, that you'll make her yours, that you'll save her: that you'll save her here temporally, and there eternally.

TEMPLAR: And how? How could I? Can I swear to do what isn't in my power?

DAJA: It is in your power. I can bring it into your power with a single word.

TEMPLAR: So that even her father would have nothing against it?

DAJA: Oh, what father? Father! Her father will have to.

TEMPLAR: Have to, Daja? He hasn't fallen among thieves. He doesn't have to have to.

DAJA: Well, he has to want to. Finally he'll have to want to gladly.

TEMPLAR: Have to and gladly! But Daja, what if I told you that I've already tried to play that tune with him?

DAJA: What? And he didn't give in?

TEMPLAR: He gave in with a sour note that ... insulted me.

DAJA: What are you saying? What? You showed him the shadow of a wish of Recha's, and he didn't jump for joy? He stepped back coldly? Made difficulties?

TEMPLAR: More or less.

DAJA: Then I won't think about it another moment. [*Pause.*]

TEMPLAR: But you're still thinking about it?

DAJA: That man is otherwise so good! I myself owe him so much! But that he should be so unwilling to listen! God knows, it breaks my heart to force him like this.

TEMPLAR: I beg you, Daja, put me out of my uncertainty once and for all. Or are you yourself still unsure whether to call what you're planning good or evil, disgraceful or praiseworthy? Just stay quiet! I want to forget that you have something to keep secret.

DAJA: That spurs, it doesn't stop. Well, know this then: Recha isn't a Jewess. She's, she's a Christian.

TEMPLAR: [*Coldly.*] So? Congratulations! Was the birth difficult? Don't be scared off by the labor pains! Go right ahead and populate heaven now that you can't do it on earth anymore!

DAJA: What, Sir knight? Does my news deserve this ridicule? That Recha is a Christian, doesn't that make you—a Christian, a Templar, and one who loves her—happy?

TEMPLAR: Oh yes, especially since she's a Christian of your making.

DAJA: Oh! So that's how you understand it? I won't hold it against you! No! I'd like to see the one who could convert her! Her luck is that she's long been what she couldn't become.

TEMPLAR: Explain yourself, or . . . leave!

DAJA: She's a Christian child, born of Christian parents, is baptized . . .

TEMPLAR: [*Quickly.*] And Nathan?

DAJA: Not her father.

TEMPLAR: Nathan's not her father? Do you know what you're saying?

DAJA: The truth, which so often made me cry bitter tears. Now, he isn't her father . . .

TEMPLAR: And he would have raised her as his own daughter? Would have raised a Christian girl as a Jewess?

DAJA: Exactly.

TEMPLAR: And she wouldn't have known what she was by birth? She wouldn't ever have learned from him that she was born a Christian and not a Jewess?

DAJA: Never!

TEMPLAR: He not only brought up the child with this delusion, but left her believing it to this day?

DAJA: Unfortunately!

TEMPLAR: Nathan, him? The wise, good Nathan would have allowed himself to falsify the voice of nature in this way? To divert the outpourings of a heart that, left alone, would have taken a completely different path? Daja, you've truly told me something of importance, which can have consequences, which has me so confused that I don't quite know what I should do next. So give me time. So go! He could come by again. He might catch us. Go!

DAJA: I would die!

TEMPLAR: At the moment I'm completely incapable of speaking to him. If you see him, just tell him that we'll meet again sometime at the Sultan's.

DAJA: But don't make him suspicious. This should just move things further in the right direction. It should take away any scruples you might have for Recha's sake! But when you take her to Europe, you won't leave me behind, will you?

TEMPLAR: We'll see about that. Just go. Go!

ACT 4

Scene 1

Scene: In the cloisters of the monastery.

The Friar and the Templar following soon thereafter.

FRIAR: Yes, yes! I suppose the Patriarch is right! I haven't been very successful with all the things he's asked me to do. But why does he ask me to do these things? I don't want to be delicate, don't want to be persuasive. I don't want to stick my nose into everything, to have my hand in everything. Is this why I separated myself from the world, I for myself, just to get tied up in the world for the sake of others?

TEMPLAR: [*Quickly coming toward him.*] Good brother! There you are. I've been looking for you for a long time.

FRIAR: Me, sir?

TEMPLAR: Don't you remember me?

FRIAR: Yes, of course! I just thought I'd never have the opportunity to see you again in my life, sir. I hoped to God I wouldn't. God knows how I hated the task that brought me to you, sir. He knows whether I hoped to find an open ear in you. He knows how happy I was, how sincerely happy, to see you completely reject everything, without giving it much thought, that didn't suit a knight. Now you're here after all; it had a delayed effect on you.   ⌄

TEMPLAR: You already know why I've come? I hardly know myself.

FRIAR: You've thought it over and decided that the Patriarch wasn't so wrong after all; that you could earn honor and money by his attack, that an enemy is an enemy, even if it was seven times an angel to us. You weighed all that with flesh and blood, and now you're back to apply for the job. Oh God!

TEMPLAR: My dear, good man! Rest assured, it's not for that reason that I've come; it's not for that reason that I want to speak to the Patriarch. I still think the same way about that point as I thought before, and for everything in the world wouldn't want to lose the good opinion that such an upright, good, dear man once honored me with. I've only come to ask the Patriarch for advice on a matter . . .

FRIAR: You're asking the advice of the Patriarch? A knight's asking advice from a . . . cleric? [*Looking around timidly.*]

TEMPLAR: Yes. It's a rather clerical matter.

FRIAR: Yet the cleric never asks the knight for advice, no matter how knightly the matter may be.

TEMPLAR: Because he has the privilege of being able to make a mistake; people like us don't envy him that. Certainly, if the matter concerned me alone, if I were only accountable to myself, what would I need your Patriarch for? But there are certain things that I'd rather have badly done by the will of another than well done by my own. Besides, I now see very well that religion is a partisan thing. And whoever thinks he's non-partisan is just holding his party's flag without realizing it. And since that's the way it is, it must be right.

FRIAR: On that I'd rather not say anything, since I don't really understand you, sir.

TEMPLAR: And yet! [*Aside:* Let's see, what should I do, really? Ask for an order or advice? For simple or scholarly advice?] I thank you, brother, thank you for the good tip. Who needs a Patriarch? You can be my Patriarch! For an adviser I'd rather have more Christian in the Patriarch than Patriarch in the Christian. This is what . . .

FRIAR: No more, sir, no more! What's the point? You misunderstand me, sir. He who knows a lot has a lot of worries. And I've only agreed to a *single* worry. Oh good! Listen! Look! Here he comes himself, thank goodness. Stay right here. He's already seen you.

Scene 2

The previous and the Patriarch, approaching the cloister with the highest degree of priestly splendor.

TEMPLAR: I'd rather avoid him. He couldn't be my man! A fat, red, friendly prelate! And what pomp!

FRIAR: You should see how he puffs himself up when he goes to court. Now he's only been to visit a sick person.

TEMPLAR: Saladin himself would be embarrassed next to him!

PATRIARCH: [*Waving to the friar as he comes closer.*] Here! That must be the Templar. What does he want?

FRIAR: Don't know.

PATRIARCH: [*Going toward him while the friar and the entourage step back.*] Now, sir knight! So happy to see the good young man! Oh, and still so young! Now, with God's help, something may come of you.

TEMPLAR: Hardly more, worthy sir, than has already come. And possibly even less.

PATRIARCH: At least I would like to see such a good knight long blossom and flourish for the honor and benefit of Christendom and the Godly cause! That won't fail to come to pass as long as young bravery carefully follows the advice of age! How else can I serve you, sir?

TEMPLAR: With the one thing I've lacked in my youth: with advice.

PATRIARCH: With pleasure! But only if the advice is also accepted.

TEMPLAR: But not blindly?

PATRIARCH: Who said that? Oh, nobody should fail to use the reason that God gave him—when appropriate. But is it always appropriate? Oh no! For example: if God deigns with the help of an angel—that is to say, with the help of a servant of his word—to make known to us a means of guaranteeing the welfare of all Christendom, the salvation of the Church in any peculiar way whatsoever, who would dare be so arbitrary as to examine according to reason Him who created reason? And to test the eternal law of Heaven's glory according to the small rules of vain honor? But enough of that. About what, then, do you need advice for now, sir?

TEMPLAR: Suppose, reverend father, that a Jew had an only child—say, a girl—whom he brought up with the greatest care for her morality, whom he loved more than his own soul, and who loved him with the most pious love. And then it would be brought to our attention that this girl wasn't the Jew's daughter; that in her infancy he had found her, bought her, stolen her, whatever you like. It would be known that the girl was a Christian, and baptized; and that the Jew had only brought her up as a Jewess, had persisted in treating her as a Jewess and as his daughter. Tell me, reverend father, what would you do in such a situation?

PATRIARCH: I'm shuddering! But first of all you must explain, sir, whether such a case is a fact or a hypothesis. That is to say, sir, if you only made this up, or if it's happened and continues to happen.

TEMPLAR: I would have thought that this wouldn't matter if the goal was to learn your highly venerable opinion.

PATRIARCH: Wouldn't matter? There, sir, you see how proud, human reason can go wrong in matters of spiritual reason. On the contrary! For if the described case is nothing but a game of the imagination, then it isn't worth thinking through seriously. I would then prefer to refer you to the theatre, sir, where such pro and con arguments are treated with much applause. But if you haven't just tried to get the best of me in a theatrical game, sir, if the case is a fact, if it indeed took place in our diocese, in our beloved city of Jerusalem, well then . . .

TEMPLAR: What then?

PATRIARCH: Then the Jew would be immediately subjected to the penalty that papal and imperial law stipulate for such a wicked deed.

TEMPLAR: And?

PATRIARCH: And the above-stated laws condemn the Jew who seduces a Christian into apostasy to the funeral pyre, the wood pile . . .

TEMPLAR: And?

PATRIARCH: And all the more so the Jew who forcibly rips a poor Christian child from the bonds of baptism! For isn't everything that one does to children force? That is to say: except what the Church does to children.

TEMPLAR: But what if the Jew's pity saved the child from dying in misery?

PATRIARCH: Doesn't matter! The Jew will be burnt! For better to die in misery here than to be rescued only for eternal ruin. Besides, who is the Jew to pre-empt God? God can save whom he wishes without him.

TEMPLAR: Or despite him, I should think.

PATRIARCH: Doesn't matter! The Jew will be burnt!

TEMPLAR: That troubles me! Especially since it's said that he brought the girl up less in his belief than in no belief, and taught her no more and no less about God than reason requires.

PATRIARCH: Doesn't matter! The Jew will be burnt . . . Indeed for this alone he would deserve to be burnt three times! What? Letting a child grow up without any belief? Not at all teaching a child the great duty of believing? That is too wicked! I'm surprised at you, sir knight . . .

TEMPLAR: Reverend sir, we'll leave the rest for confession, if God wishes. [*Wants to leave.*]

PATRIARCH: What? You won't answer my question? Won't tell me who the Jew is? Won't bring him here to me? Oh, then I know what to do! I'll go at once to the Sultan. Saladin, according to the agreement that he swore to, must protect us, and must protect us according to all the laws, all the teachings that we have always relied upon in our holiest of religions! Praise God! We have the original. We have his handwriting, his seal. We do! And I'll also show him how dangerous it is for a state when one doesn't believe anything! All civic bonds are undone, ripped to pieces, when a human being is allowed to believe nothing. Away! Away with such wickedness!

TEMPLAR: Too bad I can't enjoy the excellent sermon with more leisure! I've been called to Saladin.

PATRIARCH: Really? Well then. Well indeed. Then . . .

TEMPLAR: I'll prepare the Sultan, if it pleases Your Reverence.

PATRIARCH: Oh! Oh! I know you found favor with Saladin! Please remind him of me only in the best terms. It's only zeal for God that drives me. What I do too much, I do for Him. You'll keep that in mind, sir, won't you? And isn't it true, sir knight, that what you mentioned about the Jew was only a hypothetical problem? That is to say . . .

TEMPLAR: A hypothetical problem. [*Exit.*]

PATRIARCH: [*Aside:* I must get to the bottom of this. This would be another job for Brother Bonafides.] Here, my son! [*Speaking while walking away with the friar.*]

Scene 3

Scene: A room in Saladin's palace into which slaves carry a large quantity of bags and set them side by side on the floor.

Saladin and Sittah following shortly thereafter.

SALADIN: [*Coming forward.*] Well really! This is endless. Is there much more of the stuff coming?

A SLAVE: At least half of it.

SALADIN: Then bring the rest to Sittah. And where's Al-Hafi? Al-Hafi should take this immediately. Or maybe I should send it to father? Here it will only slip through my fingers. But one finally learns to be tough, and now it will truly take talent to get much out of me. At least until the money arrives from Egypt, the poor will have to learn how to make ends meet! If only the alms at the Holy Sepulchre can continue![37] If only the Christian pilgrims don't have to leave empty handed! If only . . .

SITTAH: What's with all this? Why am I getting all this money?

SALADIN: You're being paid, and lay aside what's left over.

SITTAH: Hasn't Nathan arrived with the Templar yet?

SALADIN: He's looking for him everywhere.

SITTAH: But look at what I found here while all these old trinkets went through my hands. [*Showing him a small painting.*]

SALADIN: Hey! My brother! It's him, it's him! It was him, was him! Oh! Oh brave, dear boy, if only I hadn't lost you so early! What I wouldn't have undertaken with you at my side! Sittah, give me the picture. I recognize it. He gave it to your older sister, his Lilla, who one morning simply wouldn't let him out of her arms. It was the last time he rode away. Oh, I let him ride, and alone! Oh, Lilla died of grief, and never forgave me for letting him ride alone like that. He didn't come back!

SITTAH: Poor brother!

SALADIN: Never mind! Eventually we all die! Eventually all of us don't come back! Besides, who knows? It's not only death that could divert a youngster like him from his goal. He had other enemies. And often the strongest succumbs to the weakest. Well, be that as it may! I still have to compare the picture with the young Templar, have to see how badly my imagination deceived me.

SITTAH: It's only for that reason that I'm bringing it. But give it to me, give it! I want to be the one to tell you. A woman's eye understands these things best.

SALADIN: [*To a gatekeeper who walks in.*] Who's there? The Templar? Let him in!

SITTAH: So I don't disturb you, so I don't confuse him with my curiosity. [*She sits down sideways on a sofa and drops a veil over her face.*]

SALADIN: That's good! Good! [*Aside:* And now his voice! I wonder what it will sound like! Assad's voice still sleeps somewhere in my soul!]

---

[37]The Holy Sepulchre is the tomb in Jerusalem in which Jesus is believed by Christians to have been buried. As stipulated in the cease-fire agreement of 1192, Christian pilgrims were permitted free access to this site under Saladin's control.

Scene 4

The Templar and Saladin.

TEMPLAR: I, your prisoner, Sultan . . .

SALADIN: My prisoner? To whomever I give life, don't I also give free-dom?

TEMPLAR: What is appropriate for you to do is for me to learn, not to presume. But, Sultan, thank you, thank you especially for vouchsaf-ing my life, though neither my stature nor my character deserves this. In any case my life is in your service again.

SALADIN: Just don't use it against me! A couple more hands I'd gladly allow my enemies. But allowing them such a heart too would be hard for me. I haven't been deceived in you, worthy young man! You are my Assad in body and soul. Look! I could ask you: Where have you been hiding the whole time? In what cave have you been sleeping? In what fairyland, thanks to what good spirit has this flower stayed so strong and fresh? Look! I could remind you of what we did together here and there. I could bicker with you about the *one* secret you kept from me, the *one* adventure you kept silent about! Yes I could do that if I only saw you and not myself too. Well, be that as it may! There's so much truth in this sweet daydream that an Assad should bloom again in the autumn of my life. Are you satisfied with this, knight?

TEMPLAR: Everything that comes from you—whatever it might be—is already a wish in my soul.

SALADIN: Then let's test that now. So you'll stay with me, and as part of my court? As Christian, as Muslim, it's all the same! In a white cloak or Jamerlonk,[38] a turban or your felt outfit. As you like it! It doesn't matter! I've never demanded that every tree grow *one* bark.

TEMPLAR: Otherwise you'd hardly be who you are: the hero who would rather be God's gardener.

SALADIN: Well then, if you don't think worse of me, then we're already halfway there?

TEMPLAR: All the way!

[38]In a letter to his brother Karl, Lessing defined *Jamerlonk* as "the broad outer gar-ment of the Arabs." *Sämtliche Schriften,* vol. 18, 313.

SALADIN: [*Offering his hand.*] Your word?

TEMPLAR: [*Shaking it.*] I'm your man! With this you'll receive more than you could take from me. I'm completely yours!

SALADIN: Too much profit for one day! Too much! Did he come with you?

TEMPLAR: Who?

SALADIN: Nathan.

TEMPLAR: [*Coldly.*] No. I came alone.

SALADIN: What a great deed you did! And what luck that such a deed made such a man so happy.

TEMPLAR: Yes, yes!

SALADIN: So cold? No, young man! When God does something good through us, we mustn't be so cold! We shouldn't even want to look so cold out of modesty!

TEMPLAR: How everything in the world has so many sides! It's often impossible to know how they all fit together!

SALADIN: Just always stick to the best side, and praise God! He knows how they fit together. But if you insist on being so difficult, young man, will I myself have to stay on my guard with you? Unfortunately I'm also a thing of many sides, which often don't seem to be able to fit together so well.

TEMPLAR: That hurts! Since suspicion is usually the least of my faults.

SALADIN: Well, then tell me, with whom do you have difficulties? Apparently with Nathan. But how? How could you be suspicious of Nathan? And you especially. Explain yourself! Speak! Come, give your trust in me a first try.

TEMPLAR: I don't have anything against Nathan. I'm only angry with myself.

SALADIN: And what about?

TEMPLAR: That I dreamt a Jew could learn how not to be a Jew, that I dreamt this while awake.

SALADIN: Out with this wakeful dream!

TEMPLAR: You know Nathan's daughter, Sultan. What I did for her I did . . . because I did it. Too proud to reap thanks where I didn't sow it, I refused day after day to see the girl again. Her father is far away. Then he comes, he hears, he seeks me out, he thanks, he wants me to like his daughter; speaks of prospects, speaks of a happy future. Now I let myself be talked into it, come, see, finally find a girl . . . Oh I should be ashamed, Sultan!

SALADIN: Ashamed? That a Jewish girl made an impression on you: are you serious?

TEMPLAR: That, encouraged by the pleasing chatter of her father, my rash heart offered so little resistance to this impression. What a fool I am! I jumped twice into the fire, since now *I* was the one to court, and now *I* was the one to be rejected.

SALADIN: Rejected?

TEMPLAR: The wise father didn't quite refuse me absolutely. But the wise father first has to make inquiries, to give it some thought. Really! Didn't I also do that? Didn't I also first make inquiries, give it some thought, when she screamed in the fire? Truly! By God! It truly is a beautiful thing to be so wise, so cautious!

SALADIN: Now, now! Don't be so hard on an old man! How long could his refusals still last? Is he going to demand that you become a Jew first?

TEMPLAR: Who knows?

SALADIN: Who knows? Anyone who knows this Nathan better.

TEMPLAR: The superstition that we grow up with doesn't lose its power over us even when we recognize it. Not everyone is free who makes fun of his chains.

SALADIN: A very mature observation! But Nathan, really, Nathan . . .

TEMPLAR: The worst superstition is the one that considers itself more justifiable than the others . . .

SALADIN: That may very well be! But Nathan . . .

TEMPLAR: To entrust the whole feeble human race to this superstition until the brighter day when the truth is revealed; to this superstition alone . . .

SALADIN: Right! But Nathan! Nathan's fate isn't to have this weakness.

TEMPLAR: That's what I thought too! But what if this paragon of humanity were such a common Jew that he would try to acquire Christian children in order to bring them up as Jews—what then?

SALADIN: Who's said such a thing about him?

TEMPLAR: The girl herself, with whom he enticed me, with whom he seemed ready to fulfill my hopes as a reward for my deed, that I shouldn't have done it in vain. This girl is not his daughter. She was an abandoned Christian child.

SALADIN: That he nevertheless didn't want to give you?

TEMPLAR: [*Sharply.*] Wants or doesn't want! He's been discovered. The tolerant chatterer has been discovered! I'll send the dogs after this Jewish wolf in philosophical sheep's clothing.

SALADIN: [*Seriously.*] Calm down, Christian!

TEMPLAR: What? Calm down, Christian? When Jew and Muslim insist on being Jew and Muslim: Should only the Christian not have the right to be a Christian?

SALADIN: [*Even more seriously.*] Calm down, Christian!

TEMPLAR: [*Calm.*] I feel the full burden of the reproach that Saladin has pressed into this word! Oh, if only I knew how Assad would have acted in my place!

SALADIN: Not much better! Presumably just as full of rage! But who taught you how you could so thoroughly charm me with *one* word? Truly if everything is as you say, I can hardly reconcile myself to such a Nathan. And yet he's my friend, and I won't allow my friends to quarrel. Take my advice. Go carefully. Don't surrender Nathan so quickly to the fanatical Christian rabble! Keep quiet about things that your clergy would ask me to avenge against him. Don't be a Christian to spite any Jew or any Muslim!

TEMPLAR: It would be almost too late for that, if the blood lust of the Patriarch hadn't revolted me so that I refused to be his tool!

SALADIN: What? You went to the Patriarch before you came to me?

TEMPLAR: In the storm of passion, in the whirlwind of indecision! Forgive me! I'm afraid you won't want to see any more of your Assad in me.

SALADIN: If it weren't this fear itself! I think I know which errors our virtue sprouts from. Just cultivate these further, and they won't cause you any more difficulty with me. But go! Look for Nathan as he looked for you, and bring him here. I have to bring the two of you to an understanding. If you're serious about the girl, be reassured. She's yours! And Nathan should be made to realize the liberties he took in raising a Christian girl without pork![39] Go! [*The Templar exits and Sittah leaves the sofa.*]

---

[39] A wry reference to the Jewish (as well as Muslim) prohibition against eating pork.

Scene 5

Saladin and Sittah.

SITTAH: Very strange!

SALADIN: Isn't it so, Sittah? Mustn't my Assad have been a worthy, beautiful young man?

SITTAH: If he was like that, and if the Templar didn't sit for this portrait! But how could you have forgotten to ask about his parents?

SALADIN: And especially about his mother? Whether his mother might never have been here in this land? Right?

SITTAH: You'll make up for that!

SALADIN: Oh, nothing would be more possible! Since Assad was so welcome with pretty Christian ladies, and so intent on pretty Christian ladies, that there was once a rumor that . . . Well, well. I'd rather not discuss that. It's enough that I have him again! I want to have him again, with all his faults, with all the moods of his tender heart! Oh! Nathan has to give him his girl. Don't you think?

SITTAH: Give him? Leave him!

SALADIN: That's right! What right does Nathan have over her if he isn't her father? The one who saved her life is the only one who can take the place of the one who gave it to her.

SITTAH: Saladin, what if you brought the girl here? If you just removed her from her unrightful owner?

SALADIN: Would that really be necessary?

SITTAH: Well, not exactly necessary! It's just my dear curiosity that drives me to suggest that. Since from certain men I like all too much and as soon as possible to know what kind of girl they could love.

SALADIN: Well, then go and send for her.

SITTAH: May I, brother?

SALADIN: But spare Nathan! Nathan must by no means believe that I would want to separate him from her by force.

SITTAH: Don't worry.

SALADIN: And I, I myself have to see where Al-Hafi is.

Scene 6

Scene: The open hall in Nathan's house, opposite the palms, as in the first scene of the first act. A portion of the wares and valuables are on display, and these are the subject of conversation.

Nathan and Daja.

DAJA: Oh, everything's splendid! Everything's choice! Everything, as only you could give it. Where was the silver cloth with the golden shoots made? What did it cost? Now that's what I call a wedding dress! No queen could ask for a better one.

NATHAN: Wedding dress? Why a wedding dress?

DAJA: Well now! Of course you weren't thinking about that when you bought it. But really, Nathan, it has to be this and no other material. It's as though you ordered it to be made into a wedding dress. The white background, a symbol of innocence; and the gold streams that weave throughout this background, a symbol of wealth. You see? Delightful!

NATHAN: Why are you joking with me like this? Whose wedding dress are you interpreting in such learned fashion? Are you the bride?

DAJA: Me?

NATHAN: Who is it then?

DAJA: Me? Dear God!

NATHAN: Who is it then? Whose wedding dress are you talking about? All this is yours and no one else's.

DAJA: It's mine? It's supposed to be mine? Isn't it for Recha?

NATHAN: What I brought for Recha is lying in another bundle. Go! Take it away! Carry your belongings away!

DAJA: Tempter! No, if they were all the treasures in the world, I wouldn't touch them! Not unless you promise me first that you'll make use of this unique opportunity, the likes of which Heaven won't send again.

NATHAN: Use? Of what? Opportunity? For what?

DAJA: Oh don't pretend you don't understand! In short: the Templar loves Recha. Give her to him, and finally your sin, which I can no longer remain silent about, will be done with. And then the girl will be among Christians again, will be again what she is; is again, what she became: and you, with all the goodness that we can't thank you enough for, you won't have just heaped coals of fire upon your head.[40]

NATHAN: Oh that old song again? Equipped with a new verse that, I'm afraid, will neither stay in tune nor hold.

DAJA: Why?

NATHAN: The Templar would be fine with me. I'd rather give Recha to him than to anyone in the world. But . . . well, just be patient.

DAJA: Patient? Now isn't patience your old song?

NATHAN: Just a few more days of patience! Look! Who's coming there? A friar? Go ask him what he wants.

DAJA: What will he want? [*She goes up to him and asks.*]

NATHAN: So give him alms, and before he asks. [*Aside:* If only I knew how to approach the Templar without telling him the reason for my curiosity! Since if I tell him, and my suspicion is groundless, then I've risked my role as father for nothing.] What is it?

DAJA: He wants to speak to you.

NATHAN: Well, then let him come. And then go.

Scene 7

Nathan and the friar.

NATHAN: [*Aside:* How I'd love to stay Recha's father! But couldn't I still be her father even if that's no longer what I'm called? To her, to her alone I'll still be "father," if she recognizes how badly I want to be her father.] Go![41] What can I do for you, good brother?

FRIAR: Not much. I'm happy, sir Nathan, to see you.

NATHAN: So you know me?

---

[40]A reference to Proverbs 25:21–22, "If thine enemy be hungry, give him bread to eat, and if he be thirsty, give him water to drink, for thou shalt heap coals of fire upon his head," and a similar command in Romans 12:20–21. Daja has taken this saying, which calls for *warm* or kind deeds, out of context, turning it into a metaphor for divine punishment. The implication is that if she is familiar with Scripture, she does not understand its meaning, a complaint that Lessing had against many contemporaries who considered themselves good Christians. This confusion is in keeping with Daja's previous sentences, which are similarly muddled.

[41]Directed at Daja.

FRIAR: Of course. Who doesn't know you? You've printed your name in the hands of so many.[42] It's remained in my hands too, for many years.

NATHAN: [*Reaching for his purse.*] Come, brother, come. I'll refresh the print.

FRIAR: No thanks! I'd be stealing from the poor. I won't take any. If only you'll allow me to refresh the print of *my* name. Then I can boast that I was able to put something worthwhile into *your* hands.

NATHAN: I beg your pardon! I'm ashamed. What were you going to say? And take as a penalty seven times the value of what you were about to give me.

FRIAR: But listen first of all to how I remembered for the first time today the pledge I entrusted to you.

NATHAN: Pledge you entrusted to me?

FRIAR: Not long ago I was a hermit on Mount Quarantana[43] near Jericho. Then a band of Arabian robbers came and destroyed my sanctuary and cell and carried me off. Luckily I escaped and ran to the Patriarch to beg him for another place where I could serve God alone until my blessed end.

NATHAN: I'm standing on coals, good brother. Make it short. The pledge! The pledge you entrusted to me!

FRIAR: Right away, sir Nathan. Now the Patriarch promised me a hermitage on Mount Tabor[44] as soon as one became available, and in the meantime ordered me to stay as a lay brother in the monastery. That's where I am now, sir Nathan, and long for Mount Tabor a hundred times a day. Because the Patriarch uses me for everything that disgusts me. For example:

NATHAN: Get to the point, I beg you!

FRIAR: Now it's coming! Someone hinted to him that somewhere around here is a Jew who raised a Christian child as his daughter.

NATHAN: What? [*Taken aback.*]

---

[42]That is, by giving alms.

[43]Named after the desert in which, according to Christian belief, Jesus spent his forty days of temptation.

[44]Mount Tabor is where Christians believe the Transfiguration of Christ occurred.

FRIAR: Just let me finish! While he was ordering me to track down this Jew right away, if possible, and growing angry at such an outrage, which seems to him the true sin against the Holy Spirit—that is, the sin which of all sins counts for us as the greatest sin, though, thank God, we don't quite know what it actually consists of[45]—suddenly my conscience woke up and it occurred to me that I myself might have been the one who long ago provided the opportunity for this unforgivably great sin. Say, didn't a horseman bring you a little daughter, a few weeks old, eighteen years ago.

NATHAN: What? Yes, truly—really . . .

FRIAR: Hey, look at me carefully! That horseman's me.

NATHAN: It's you?

FRIAR: The man I brought her from was a Herr von Filnek. Wolf von Filnek!

NATHAN: Right!

FRIAR: Since the mother had just recently died and the father had to rush, I believe, to Gaza,[46] where the little baby couldn't follow, he sent her to you. And didn't I meet you with her in Darum?[47]

NATHAN: Exactly!

FRIAR: It wouldn't be a wonder if my memory deceived me. I've had so many worthy masters, and I only served this one for such a short time. He died at Ascalon,[48] and was a kind man.

NATHAN: Yes indeed! Yes indeed! I have so many, many reasons to be grateful to him! More than once he saved me from the sword!

FRIAR: Wonderful! Then you must have been all the happier to take his little daughter.

NATHAN: You can imagine.

---

[43]Named after the desert in which, according to Christian belief, Jesus spent his forty days of temptation.

[44]Mount Tabor is where Christians believe the Transfiguration of Christ occurred.

[45]This is a parody of the type of reasoning that Lessing believed many orthodox Christians used in their theological speculations.

[46]An ancient Mediterranean city in southern Palestine. It was conquered by Crusaders in 1100, then retaken by Saladin in 1170.

[47]A fortress south of Gaza on the Mediterranean.

[48]Ascalon (Ashkelon) was a Mediterranean city in southern Palestine (today Israel), just north of Gaza.

FRIAR: Well, where is she then? She hasn't died, has she? Don't let her be dead! And if no one else knows about the matter, everything will be alright.

NATHAN: Alright?

FRIAR: Trust me, Nathan! Look, this is how I see it. When something all too evil borders all too closely on the good that I think I'm doing, then I'd rather not do that good thing. Because we can more or less count on the evil, but not at all on the good. It was only natural, if you were going to bring up the little Christian daughter properly, that you would bring her up as your own daughter. That you would have done so out of love and fidelity, and this should be your reward? I don't think so. Oh really, if you had been smarter you would have let the Christian girl be raised as a Christian girl by someone else. But then you wouldn't have loved your friend's little child. And at that age children need love, if only the love of a wild animal, more than Christianity. For Christianity there's always time. As long as the girl grew up healthy and pious in your eyes, she remains in God's eyes what she was. And isn't all of Christianity built on Judaism? It's often angered me, it's cost me enough tears to see Christians forget so completely that our Lord himself was a Jew.

NATHAN: You, good brother, should be my advocate if hatred and hypocrisy rise up against me—on account of a deed—oh, on account of a deed! Only you, you alone will know of it! But take it with you to the grave! Vanity has never tempted me to tell anyone else. I'll tell only you. I'll tell only pious simplicity, since only that understands what deeds a human being devoted to God can bring himself to do.

FRIAR: You're moved, and your eyes are full of water?

NATHAN: You met me with the child at Darum. But what you didn't know was that a few days earlier, in Gath,[49] the Christians had murdered all the Jews—men, women, and children—and you didn't know that among these were my wife and seven hopeful sons, whom I had sent to take refuge in my brother's house, and who all burned to death there.

FRIAR: God of Justice!

---

[49] A Mediterranean city in the vicinity of Ascalon.

NATHAN: When you came I had lain before God for three days and nights in ashes and dust, and cried. Cried? Reckoned with God, was angry at him, raged against him, cursed myself and the world, swore the most unforgiving hatred of Christendom . . .

FRIAR: Oh I can believe you!

NATHAN: But then reason came back gradually. It said with a gentle voice, "And yet God exists! This too was God's decree! Now then! Come! Practice what you've long understood, what is surely no more difficult to practice than it is to understand, if only you want to. Stand up!" I stood! And I called to God, "I want to! If only you want me to want to!" Meanwhile you came down from your horse and handed me the child, wrapped in your coat. What you said to me, what I said to you, I've forgotten. All I know is this: I took the child, carried her back to my couch, kissed her, threw myself on my knees and sobbed, "God! For seven at least you've given me back one!"

FRIAR: Nathan! Nathan! You're a Christian! By God, you're a Christian! There never was a better Christian!

NATHAN: That's well for us! For what makes me a Christian to you makes you a Jew to me! But let's not just move each other. We have to do something! And though sevenfold love quickly bound me to this single foreign girl, though the thought kills me that in her I should lose my seven sons again, if Providence orders her out of my hands again—I'll obey!

FRIAR: Exactly! That's just what I thought of advising you to do! And your own good mind already guessed it!

NATHAN: It's just that she mustn't be carried off by the first to claim her!

FRIAR: No, certainly not!

NATHAN: Whoever doesn't have more of a right to her than I should at least have prior rights . . .

FRIAR: Absolutely!

NATHAN: Given by nature and blood.

FRIAR: I think so too!

NATHAN: So quickly tell me the name of her brother or uncle or cousin or other male relative. I won't hold her back from him. She was made and raised to be the jewel of any family, of any religion. I hope you know more about this man and his family than I do.

FRIAR: That, good Nathan, I can hardly do! You've just heard that I was with him for far too short a time.

NATHAN: Don't you at least know what family her mother came from? Wasn't she a Stauffen?

FRIAR: Quite possibly! Yes, it seems to me she was.

NATHAN: Wasn't her brother Conrad von Stauffen? And a Templar?

FRIAR: If I'm not mistaken. But wait! I just remembered that I still have a little book from the blessed man. I took it from his breast pocket when we buried him at Ascalon.

NATHAN: And?

FRIAR: There are prayers in it. We call it a breviary. I thought a Christian could make good use of it. Of course I couldn't. I can't read.

NATHAN: Doesn't matter! Just get to the point.

FRIAR: In this little book my master wrote, in the front and the back, with his own hand, I've been told, the names of his relatives and hers.

NATHAN: Oh wonderful! Go! Run! Get me the little book. Quickly! I'm prepared to pay its weight in gold. And a thousand thanks too! Hurry! Run!

FRIAR: I'll be glad to! But what my master wrote is in Arabic. [*Exit.*]

NATHAN: That doesn't matter! Just bring it here! God! If I could only keep the girl and get such a son-in-law in the bargain! That's hardly likely! Well, come what will! But who could it have been who told the Patriarch? I mustn't forget to ask that. I wonder if it was Daja.

Scene 8

Daja and Nathan.

DAJA: [*Hurrying and embarrassed.*] Just think, Nathan!

NATHAN: Yes?

DAJA: The poor child really got a scare! A message from . . .

NATHAN: The Patriarch?

DAJA: The Sultan's sister, Princess Sittah . . .

NATHAN: Not the Patriarch?

DAJA: No. Sittah! Can't you hear? Princess Sittah has sent a message and is having her brought to her.

NATHAN: Who? Having Recha brought to her? Sittah's having her brought to her? Well, if it's Sittah, and not the Patriarch . . .

DAJA: What made you think of him?

NATHAN: So you haven't recently heard anything from him? You're sure you haven't? And you haven't told him anything?

DAJA: Me? Him?

NATHAN: Where are the messengers?

DAJA: In front.

NATHAN: I want to speak to them, just to make sure. Come! I just hope the Patriarch isn't behind any of this. [*Exit.*]

DAJA: And I—I'm afraid of something completely different. It seems the supposed only daughter of such a rich Jew isn't so bad for a Muslim. That's it. The Templar has lost her. Lost her, unless I dare to take the second step and reveal to her who she is! Don't worry! Let me make use of the first moment when I have her alone! And that moment will come, perhaps right now if I accompany her. At least a first hint on the way can't hurt. Yes, yes! Do it! Now or never! Do it! [*After him.*]

ACT 5

Scene 1

Scene: The room in Saladin's palace into which the money bags, which are still visible, have been carried.

Saladin and various Mamelukes following shortly thereafter.

SALADIN: [*Stepping in.*] Well, the money's still sitting there! And no one knows where to find the dervish, who presumably got so involved with the chessboard that he forgot himself. Why shouldn't he have forgotten me too? Just be patient! What is it?

MAMELUKE: Good news, Sultan! Wonderful, Sultan! The Caravan from Cairo has come, it's safely arrived! And with seven years' tribute from the rich Nile.

SALADIN: Good, Ibrahim! You're truly a welcome messenger! Ah! Finally! Finally! Thank you for the good news.

MAMELUKE: [*Waiting.*] [*Aside:* Well? Let's have it!]

SALADIN: What are you waiting for? You can go now.

MAMELUKE: Nothing else for the welcome messenger?

SALADIN: What do you mean?

MAMELUKE: No tip for the good messenger? Then I'll be the first person Saladin ever learned to reward with words? That's also an honor! The first one he was ever stingy to.

SALADIN: Then take a bag for yourself.

MAMELUKE: No, not now! You could try to give them all to me now. Forget about it.

SALADIN: Stubborn, are you! Here, take two. Is he serious? He's leaving? He's trying to outdo me in nobility? After all, it must be harder for him to refuse me than for me to give to him. Ibrahim! What was I thinking: to become a completely different person so shortly before my departure? Doesn't Saladin want to die as Saladin? Then mustn't he live as Saladin?

SECOND MAMELUKE: Well, Sultan!

SALADIN: If you're coming to tell me . . .

SECOND MAMELUKE: That the shipment from Egypt has come!

SALADIN: I already know.

SECOND MAMELUKE: Then I've come too late!

SALADIN: Why too late? For your good intentions take a bag or two.

SECOND MAMELUKE: Make it three!

SALADIN: Yes, if you know how to count! Just take them.

SECOND MAMELUKE: A third messenger should come, that is, if he manages to make it.

SALADIN: Why shouldn't he?

SECOND MAMELUKE: Well, he might have broken his neck! Since as soon as we three learned of the arrival of the shipment, everyone left in a hurry. The first one crashed, and so I arrived first in the city, but Ibrahim, the scoundrel, knows his way around the streets better than I do.

SALADIN: Oh, the one who crashed! Friend, the one who crashed! Ride to him at once.

SECOND MAMELUKE: I'll do that! And if he's alive then half of this bag is his. [*Exit.*]

SALADIN: What a good, noble fellow he is! Who else can boast of such Mamelukes? And would I be wrong to think that my example helped to make them this way? Don't even think about getting them used to a different example!

THIRD MAMELUKE: Sultan . . .

SALADIN: Are you the one who crashed?

THIRD MAMELUKE: No. I'm just here to report that Emir Mansor, who led the caravan, is dismounting . . .

SALADIN: Bring him here! Quickly! There he is now!

Scene 2

Emir Mansor and Saladin.

SALADIN: Welcome, Emir! Well, how did it go? Mansor, Mansor, you've left us waiting so long!

EMIR MANSOR: This letter reports what unrest your Abulkassem had to quell in Thebais[50] before we dared leave. I tried to speed the caravan as much as possible.

SALADIN: I believe you! And now, good Mansor, take immediately . . . You'll do so gladly, won't you? Take a fresh convoy immediately. You must go further. You must bring the greater part of the money to my father in Lebanon.

EMIR MANSOR: Gladly! Very gladly!

SALADIN: And see to it that your convoy isn't too weak. Things in Lebanon aren't so secure anymore. Haven't you heard? The Templars are moving again. Be on your guard! Come now! Where's the caravan? I want to see it and manage everything myself. Hey, you! I'll be with Sittah in a minute.

Scene 3

Scene: The palms in front of Nathan's house, where the Templar walks back and forth.

TEMPLAR: I don't want to go into his house. He's sure to show up sooner or later. I used to be noticed so quickly, so happily! Now I wouldn't be surprised if he didn't let me spend so much time in front of his house. Hm! I'm still rather angry. But what is it that made me so bitter toward him? He said he wouldn't refuse me any-

---

[50]Abulkassem is apparently a fictional character. The uprising to which the Emir refers is imagined. Thebais, named for its principal city of Thebes, is the region also known as Upper Egypt.

thing. And Saladin has taken it upon himself to influence him in my favor. So? Could the Christian really be more deeply rooted in me than the Jew is in him? Who has such self-knowledge? How could I begrudge him the little theft he committed, under such circumstances, against a Christian? Of course, it was no small bundle of loot, such a creature! Creature? And whose? Does she belong to the slave who cast the block onto the desolate shore of life and then left? Doesn't she much more rightfully belong to the artist who traced the divine form into the abandoned block? Oh! Recha's true father remains—despite the Christian who engendered her— remains forever the Jew. When I simply think of her as a Christian girl without thinking of everything I believe such a Jew was able to give her: tell me, heart! What about her would please you? Nothing! Hardly anything! Even her smile would be nothing but the gentle, pretty pulling of her muscles. What made her smile, as it clothed itself in her mouth, would be unworthy of the impulse. No, not even her smile! I've seen much more beautiful smiles wasted on foolishness, on nonsense, on ridicule, on flatterers and lovers! Did they enchant me then? Did they draw from me the wish to spend my life fluttering in their sunshine? I should think not. And yet I'm angry at the one who alone gave her this higher worth? How could that be? Why? Perhaps I deserved the ridicule that Saladin dismissed me with! It's bad enough that Saladin could believe it! How small I must have seemed to him! How contemptible! And all that for a girl? Curd! Curd! That won't do. Turn around! And what if Daja just blathered something that can hardly be proved? Look, there he is stepping out of his house, absorbed in conversation! Oh! With whom? With him? With my friar? Oh! Then he must know everything! He's been betrayed to the Patriarch! Oh! What a blockhead I am! What have I done? How a single spark of passion can burn so much of one's brain! I must quickly decide what to do now! I'll hide here and watch them. Maybe the friar will leave.

Scene 4

Nathan and the Friar.

NATHAN: [*Coming nearer.*] Thank you again, good brother!

FRIAR: And the same to you!

NATHAN: Me? From you? What for? For my obstinacy in forcing onto you what you don't need? If only my obstinacy hadn't yielded to yours, if only you hadn't wanted so forcefully to be richer than I am.[51]

FRIAR: Besides, the book doesn't belong to me. It belongs to the daughter. It's the daughter's entire inheritance from her father, so to speak. Now, of course, she has you. May God only grant that you never regret having done so much for her!

NATHAN: Can I do that? I can never do that! Don't worry!

FRIAR: Now, now! The Patriarchs and the Templars . . .

NATHAN: Could never do me so much harm that I would regret anything, let alone that! And are you absolutely sure it was a Templar who's been stirring up your Patriarch?

FRIAR: It could hardly be anyone else. A Templar spoke with him shortly beforehand, and what I heard sounded like this.

NATHAN: But there is now only one Templar in Jerusalem. And this one I know. This one is my friend. A young, noble, sincere man!

FRIAR: Quite right, he's the one! But what one is, and what one has to be in the world, these don't always fit together.

NATHAN: Unfortunately not. So let him, whoever he may be, do his worst or his best! With your book, brother, I'll stand up to anyone, and I'll go straight to the Sultan with it.

FRIAR: Good luck! So I'll leave you here.

NATHAN: And without having seen her even once? Just come quickly, just come again often. If only the Patriarch hasn't heard anything yet! But what does that matter? Tell him today whatever you like.

FRIAR: I won't. Farewell! [*Exit.*]

NATHAN: Don't forget us, brother! God! If only I could fall down on my knees right here and now in the open air! How the knot that so often made me afraid is now loosening by itself! God! How light I'm becoming now that I have nothing left on earth to hide! Now that I can walk so freely before human beings as I do before you, who alone do not have to judge human beings by their deeds, which so rarely are their deeds, oh God!

---

[51]Nathan means that by refusing Nathan's charity, the friar became morally or spiritually richer.

Scene 5

Nathan and the Templar coming up to him from the side.

TEMPLAR: Hey! Wait, Nathan. Take me with you!

NATHAN: Who's calling? Is it you, knight? Where were you that I couldn't meet you at the Sultan's?

TEMPLAR: We missed each other. No offense.

NATHAN: None taken. But Saladin . . .

TEMPLAR: You had just left . . .

NATHAN: Then you did speak to him? Well then, everything's okay.

TEMPLAR: But he wants to speak to both of us together.

NATHAN: All the better. Just come with me. I was on my way to him.

TEMPLAR: May I ask you, Nathan, who just left you?

NATHAN: But don't you know him?

TEMPLAR: Wasn't that the good fellow, the lay brother the Patriarch likes so much to use as a spy?

NATHAN: Maybe! He is in the Patriarch's service.

TEMPLAR: That's not a bad trick, sending simplicity before committing villainy.

NATHAN: Yes, if the simple one is stupid, not pious.

TEMPLAR: No Patriarch believes in piety.

NATHAN: I can vouch for this one. He would never help the Patriarch carry out anything improper.

TEMPLAR: At least that's how he acts. But didn't he say anything to you about me?

NATHAN: About you? He didn't say anything about you by name. After all, he hardly knows your name.

TEMPLAR: Hardly.

NATHAN: It's true, he did say something to me about a Templar . . .

TEMPLAR: And what?

NATHAN: Something that couldn't possibly have applied to you.

TEMPLAR: Who knows? Let's hear.

NATHAN: That someone accused me before the Patriarch . . .

TEMPLAR: Accused you? That is, no offense to him, a lie. Listen to me, Nathan! I'm not the sort of person who's inclined to deny anything he's done. What I did, I did! But I'm also not the sort of person who wants to justify everything he's done as a good deed. Why should I be ashamed of a fault? Don't I have the firm resolve to correct it? And don't I know how far such resolve can take people? Listen to me, Nathan! I really am the Templar the lay brother was talking about, the one who supposedly accused you. Now you know what made me angry! What made my blood boil in all its veins! What a fool I am! I came to throw myself so completely with body and soul into your arms. The way you received me, so cold, so lukewarm (and lukewarm is worse than cold). How diligently reserved you were as you turned away from me. How you answered me with questions that seemed to come out of thin air. I can hardly think about it even now when I ought to be calm. Listen to me, Nathan! While I was so agitated, Daja crept up behind me and hit me on the head with the secret that seemed to contain the explanation for your mysterious behavior.

NATHAN: How's that?

TEMPLAR: Let me finish! I imagined that you didn't want to lose again to a Christian what you once rescued from a Christian. And so it occurred to me to place the knife at your throat. That's the story, nice and short.

NATHAN: Nice and short? Nice? Where's the nice part?

TEMPLAR: Listen to me, Nathan! It's true, what I did wasn't right! You're not in the least guilty. That fool Daja doesn't know what she's talking about. She's spiteful toward you, only wants to get you in trouble. Maybe! Maybe! I'm a young fool who goes from one extreme to the other. I either do too much or too little. That too may be the case! Forgive me, Nathan.

NATHAN: If you put it that way, certainly . . .

TEMPLAR: In short, I went to the Patriarch! But didn't name you. That's a lie, as I said! I only told him of the case in general terms to get his opinion. That too didn't have to take place, I admit it! After all, didn't I already know the Patriarch was a scoundrel? Couldn't I have gone straight to you to hear what you had to say? Did I have to put the poor girl in danger of losing such a father? Well, what does that matter? The Patriarch's vile nature, which always remains the same, quickly brought me back to myself. Listen to me, Nathan! Let me finish! Supposing he did know your name, what then? What then? He can only take the girl from you when she doesn't belong to anyone but you. He can only drag her out of *your* house into a convent. So—give her to me! Just give her to me, and let him come. Ha! He won't dare take my wife away from me. Give her to me, quickly! Whether she's really your daughter or not! Whether she's Christian or Jewish or nothing! It doesn't matter! It doesn't matter! I'll never ask you about it again in my entire life, neither now nor ever. It doesn't matter!

NATHAN: Do you imagine it's important to me to conceal the truth?

TEMPLAR: It doesn't matter!

NATHAN: I've never denied to you or anyone else who was fit to know that she's a Christian and only my adoptive daughter. But why I haven't let her know, it's only to her that I have to explain that.

TEMPLAR: You shouldn't even have to explain that to her. Allow her never to see you with different eyes! Spare her the discovery! You're still the one, the only one who's in charge of her. Give her to me! I beg you, Nathan. Give her to me! I'm the only one who can and will save her a second time.

NATHAN: Yes, could have! Could have! But can't anymore. For that it's too late.

TEMPLAR: Why too late?

NATHAN: Thanks to the Patriarch . . .

TEMPLAR: The Patriarch? Thanks? Thanks to him? What for? How could *he* deserve our thanks? What for? What for?

NATHAN: That we now know whom she's related to, now know whom she can safely be handed over to.

TEMPLAR: Let the Devil thank the Patriarch. He has other things to thank him for as well!

NATHAN: From these relatives' hands you too must receive her, and not from mine.

TEMPLAR: Poor Recha! What you have to endure! What would be lucky for another orphan is your misfortune! Nathan! And where are they, these relatives?

NATHAN: Where are they?

TEMPLAR: And who are they?

NATHAN: In particular a brother has turned up, and you need to ask him for her.

TEMPLAR: A brother? What is he, this brother? A soldier? A priest? Let's hear what I have to expect.

NATHAN: I think he's neither of the two, or both. I don't know him well yet.

TEMPLAR: And what else?

NATHAN: A good man whom Recha won't be badly off with.

TEMPLAR: But a Christian! Right now I still don't know what to think of you. Don't take it the wrong way, Nathan. But won't she have to play the Christian among Christians? And won't she finally become what she's played long enough? Won't the weeds finally suffocate the pure wheat that you've sown? And you care so little about that? Despite that you, *you* can say that she won't be badly off with her brother?

NATHAN: I think so! I hope so! And if she should be lacking anything with him, won't she always have you and me?

TEMPLAR: Oh, what could she be lacking with him? Won't the dear brother provide his dear sister with plenty of food and clothing, good food and fine clothing? And what more could a dear sister want?[52] Of course, a husband too! Well, well, that too, that too the dear brother will find in time; if he can be found. The more Christian, the better! Nathan, Nathan! What an angel you've formed to be spoiled by the poor craftsmanship of others!

NATHAN: There's no risk of that! He'll show himself to be worthy of our love.

TEMPLAR: Don't say that! Don't say that about *my* love! Mine isn't suppressed by anything, anything, however little! Not even by names! But wait! Does she suspect at all what's happening to her?

NATHAN: It's possible, though I wouldn't know how.

TEMPLAR: It doesn't matter. In any case she should, she must learn from me first what threatens her fate. I've given up the idea that I wouldn't see her or speak to her until I had the right to call her mine. I have to hurry . . .

NATHAN: Wait! Where?

---

[52]Rather than using the normal terms for brother (*Bruder*) and sister (*Schwester*), the Templar uses the diminutives *Brüderchen* and *Schwesterchen*. These untranslatable terms—"brotherlet" and "sisterlet" are not words in English—suggest affection, but in the context of the Templar's anger they are clearly being used sarcastically.

TEMPLAR: To her! To see if this girl's soul is truly brave enough to make the only decision worthy of it!

NATHAN: *Which* decision?

TEMPLAR: This one: not to ask either you or her brother.

NATHAN: And?

TEMPLAR: And to follow me, even if she should have to become the wife of a Muslim.[53]

NATHAN: Wait! You won't find her. She's with Sittah, the Sultan's sister.

TEMPLAR: Since when? Why?

NATHAN: And if you want to meet the brother at the same time, just come with me.

TEMPLAR: The brother? Which one? Sittah's or Recha's?

NATHAN: Maybe both. Just come with me! Please, come! [*He leads him away.*]

Scene 6

Scene: In Sittah's harem.

Sittah and Recha engaged in conversation.

SITTAH: How happy I am for you, sweet girl! Don't be so anxious, so afraid, so shy! Be cheerful! Be more talkative, more comfortable!

RECHA: Princess . . .

SITTAH: But no! Not "princess"! Call me Sittah, your friend, your sister. Call me Mom! I could be your mother, after all. So young! So bright! So good! What don't you know? What haven't you read?

RECHA: Read? Sittah, you're making fun of your silly little sister. I can hardly read.

SITTAH: Can hardly read? You're lying!

RECHA: A little of my father's handwriting! I thought you were talking about books.

SITTAH: Absolutely! About books.

RECHA: Well, it's really hard for me to read books!

SITTAH: Seriously?

---

[53]The Templar means that he is willing to become a Muslim if the Sultan requires him to before allowing him to marry Recha.

RECHA: Quite seriously. My father isn't too fond of cold book-learning, which only impresses dead signs into the brain.

SITTAH: Oh, what are you saying? On the other hand he's not entirely wrong. And yet you know so much . . .

RECHA: I only know what came from his mouth, and for most of these things I could tell you how, where, and why he taught them to me.

SITTAH: So everything holds together better. So you learn with your entire soul.

RECHA: Certainly you haven't read much if at all!

SITTAH: Why? I'm not proud to say the opposite. But why? What are your reasons? Speak openly. Your reasons?

RECHA: You're so modest, so unpretentious, so completely yourself . . .

SITTAH: Well?

RECHA: My father says books rarely allow us to be that way.

SITTAH: Oh what a man your father is!

RECHA: Isn't it true?

SITTAH: How close to the mark he always hits!

RECHA: Isn't it true? And yet, this father . . .

SITTAH: What's the matter, dear?

RECHA: This father . . .

SITTAH: God! You're crying?

RECHA: And this father . . . Oh! It has to come out! My heart needs air, needs air . . . [*Overcome with tears, throws herself at Sittah's feet.*]

SITTAH: Child, what's happening to you? Recha?

RECHA: This father . . . I'm going to lose!

SITTAH: You? Lose? Him? How's that? Calm down! Never! Stand up!

RECHA: You shouldn't have offered in vain to be my friend, my sister!

SITTAH: But I am! I am! Just stand up! Otherwise I'll have to call for help.

RECHA: [*Pulling herself together and standing up.*] Oh, pardon me! Forgive me! My pain made me forget who you are. Sittah doesn't allow crying or desperation. Only cold, calm reason carries weight with her. Whoever uses this in pleading his case to her wins!

SITTAH: Well then?

RECHA: No. My friend, my sister will never allow this! Will never allow me to be forced onto another father!

SITTAH: Another father? Forced upon you? Who could do that? Who would want to do that, dear?

RECHA: Who? My good, evil Daja could want to do that, claims to be able to do that. Well, don't you know this good, evil Daja? God forgive her for this! Reward her for the other things! She has proved herself capable of so much good and so much evil toward me!

SITTAH: Evil toward you? Then she must truly have little good in her.

RECHA: On the contrary! She has quite a lot. Quite a lot!

SITTAH: Who is she?

RECHA: A Christian woman who cared for me in my childhood, who cared for me so well—you won't believe me—that I hardly regretted not having a mother! God bless her for that! But who also frightened and tormented me so badly!

SITTAH: And over what? Why? How?

RECHA: Oh! The poor woman—let me tell you—is a Christian, has to torment out of love. She's one of those fanatics who imagine they know the universal and only true path to God!

SITTAH: Now I understand!

RECHA: And who feel compelled to lead everyone who strays from this path back onto it. But she could hardly do otherwise. After all, if it's true that this is the only true path, how could we allow her to see her friends walk another one, one that leads to ruin, to eternal ruin? It would have to be possible to love and hate the same person at the same time. But it isn't this that's finally forced me to complain so openly about her. I could have gladly endured even longer her sighs, her warnings, her praying, her threats. Gladly! That always brought me to good and useful thoughts. And who isn't flattered to feel so worthy and dear to someone that this person cannot bear the thought of having to give one up forever?

SITTAH: Very true!

RECHA: Only, only, *that's* going too far! I can't offer any resistance to that. No patience, no consideration, nothing!

SITTAH: What? To what?

RECHA: What she just now revealed to me.

SITTAH: Revealed? And just now?

RECHA: Just now! On the way here we came to a ruined Christian chapel. Suddenly she stood still, seemed to be struggling with herself, looked with moist eyes toward heaven, then toward me.

"Come," she finally said. "Let's take a shortcut through this chapel." She goes, I follow her, and my eyes sweep with dread through the tottering ruins. Now she stops again, and I find myself with her on the sunken steps of a rotting altar. How I felt when she fell to my feet with hot tears and wringing her hands . . .

SITTAH: Poor child!

RECHA: And swore by the Virgin Mary, who had answered so many other prayers and performed so many miracles—swore with a look of true sympathy—to have pity on me! And asked her forgiveness for having to reveal to me the claims that her church had on me.

SITTAH: [*Aside:* The poor thing! I suspected as much!]

RECHA: She told me that I was of Christian blood, that I was baptized, that I wasn't Nathan's daughter, that he wasn't my father! God! God! That he's not my father! Sittah! Sittah! Look, I'm at your feet again . . .

SITTAH: Recha! No! Stand up! My brother's coming! Stand up!

Scene 7

Saladin and the previous.

SALADIN: What's going on here, Sittah?

SITTAH: She's beside herself! God!

SALADIN: Who is it?

SITTAH: You know, don't you?

SALADIN: Our Nathan's daughter? What's the matter with her?

SITTAH: Get a hold of yourself, child! The Sultan . . .

RECHA: [*Dragging herself on her knees to Saladin's feet, her head sunk toward the ground.*] I won't stand up! Won't stand up unless—don't want to see his face unless—don't want to admire the reflection of eternal righteousness and goodness in his eyes and on his brow . . .

SALADIN: Stand . . . stand up!

RECHA: Unless he promises me . . .

SALADIN: Come! I promise . . . whatever it may be!

RECHA: No more, no less, than to let me keep my father, and to let him keep me! I still don't know who else claims, or can claim, to be my father. Nor do I want to know. But is it only blood that makes the father? Only blood?

SALADIN: [*Lifting her up.*] I understand! Who was so cruel as to put such ideas into your head, into *your* head? Is it certain? Has it been proved?

RECHA: Must have been! Since Daja claims to know it from my wet nurse.

SALADIN: From your wet nurse!

RECHA: Who, while she was dying, felt compelled to entrust it to her.

SALADIN: Just dying! And not raving too? And even if it were true! Truly blood, blood alone does not make the father! It hardly makes the father of an animal! At the most it confers the right to earn that name! Don't be afraid! And do you know what? As soon as two fathers start to fight over you, leave both of them. Take the third! Take me as your father!

SITTAH: Oh do it! Do it!

SALADIN: I want to be a good father, a really good father! But wait! I've just thought of something better. Why do you need fathers at all? What if they were to die? Why not look for a man who stands to outlive us? Don't you know any?

SITTAH: Don't make her blush!

SALADIN: That was precisely my intention. Blushing makes the ugly so beautiful. Shouldn't it make the beautiful even more beautiful? I've sent for your father Nathan and another man as well. Can you guess who he is? Come here! With your permission, Sittah?

SITTAH: Brother!

SALADIN: May you blush quite a bit when you see him, dear girl!

RECHA: When I see whom? Blush?

SALADIN: Don't be coy! Okay, then, go pale if you prefer! As you like, and can! [*A slave woman enters and approaches Sittah.*] Aren't they here yet?

SITTAH: [*To the slave woman.*] Good, just let them in. There they are, brother!

Final Scene

Enter Nathan and the Templar.

SALADIN: Ah, my good, dear friends! You, you, Nathan, I must tell you first of all that you can have your money back as soon as you like!

NATHAN: Sultan!

SALADIN: Now I'm at your service . . .

NATHAN: Sultan!

SALADIN: The caravan is here. I'm richer now than I've been in a long time. Come, tell me what you need to undertake something big! After all, you business people can never have too much cash!

NATHAN: But why start off with this trifle? I see here eyes in tears; to dry them is much more important to me. [*goes to Recha*] You've been crying? What's the matter? Aren't you still my daughter?

RECHA: My father!

NATHAN: We understand each other. Enough! Be happy! Be calm! As long as your heart is still yours! As long as no other loss threatens your heart! You haven't lost your father!

RECHA: None, no other!

TEMPLAR: No other? Well, then I've deceived myself! What you've never been afraid of losing you've never thought nor wished to have. Just fine! Just fine! That changes everything, Nathan! Saladin, we came here at your command. But I misled you. Now I won't trouble you any further!

SALADIN: There you go losing your temper again, young man! Does everything have to go your way? Does everyone have to guess your thoughts?

TEMPLAR: But don't you hear? Don't you see, Sultan?

SALADIN: Oh yes! It's bad enough that you weren't surer of your case!

TEMPLAR: I am now.

SALADIN: Whoever takes advantage of a good deed hasn't done a good deed after all. What you've saved isn't for that reason your property. If it were, then the robber who ran after his loot in a fire would be as good a hero as you! [*Going to Recha to lead her to the Templar.*] Come, dear girl, come! Don't take him so literally. After all, if he weren't so hot-tempered and proud he wouldn't have bothered to save you. You have to count one deed against the other. Come, shame him! Do what's appropriate to him! Admit your love for him! Propose to him! And if he rejects you, if he ever forgets how much more you've done for him in this step than he ever did for you— What did he do for you? Got a little smoky. Bravo!—if he mistreats you in this way then he has nothing of my brother Assad, nothing!

Then he only wears his shell and doesn't have his heart. Come, dear . . .

SITTAH: Go, go dear! Go! It's hardly anything considering your gratitude; it's really nothing.

NATHAN: Stop, Saladin! Stop, Sittah!

SALADIN: You too?

NATHAN: There's another person who needs to be consulted about this.

SALADIN: Who would deny that? Undeniably such a foster father should have a say in this! The first, if you like. You see, I know the whole state of affairs.

NATHAN: Not completely! I'm not talking about myself. There's another person. Another person altogether, Saladin, whose voice I would first like to hear.

SALADIN: Who?

NATHAN: Her brother!

SALADIN: Recha's brother?

NATHAN: Yes!

RECHA: My brother? So I have a brother?

TEMPLAR: [*Coming out of his wild, mute distraction.*] Where? Where is he, this brother? Not here yet? I'm supposed to meet him here.

NATHAN: Just be patient!

TEMPLAR: [*Very bitterly.*] He already imposed a father on her. Is it surprising he should find a brother too?

SALADIN: That's the last straw! Christian! Such a vile suspicion would never have come across my Assad's lips. Anyway! Continue!

NATHAN: Forgive him! I'm happy to forgive him. Who knows what we would think in his place and at his age! [*Going up to him in a friendly manner.*] Of course, knight! Mild mistrust leads to real suspicion! If only you had told me your *real* name right away . . .

TEMPLAR: What?

NATHAN: You're not a Stauffen!

TEMPLAR: Then who am I?

NATHAN: Your name isn't Curd von Stauffen!

TEMPLAR: What is my name, then?

NATHAN: Your name is Leu von Filnek.

TEMPLAR: What?

NATHAN: You're surprised?

TEMPLAR: Shouldn't I be? Who says that's my name?

NATHAN: I do, and I can tell you even more. Now I'm not accusing you of lying.

TEMPLAR: You're not?

NATHAN: It's still possible that you have a right to that name too.

TEMPLAR: I should hope so! [*Aside:* He's lucky God made him say that!]

NATHAN: Because your mother, she was a Stauffen. Her brother, your uncle, who raised you, whom your parents left you with in Germany when that raw climate drove them back to this country—he was called Curd von Stauffen. He may even have adopted you! Has it been a long time since you came over here with him? And is he still alive?

TEMPLAR: What should I say? Nathan! That's right! It is! He himself is dead. I first came here with the last reinforcements of our order. But, but . . . what does all this have to do with Recha's brother?

NATHAN: Your father . . .

TEMPLAR: What? You knew him too? Him too?

NATHAN: He was my friend.

TEMPLAR: Your friend? Is it possible, Nathan!

NATHAN: His name was Wolf von Filnek, but he wasn't a German . . .

TEMPLAR: You know that too?

NATHAN: He was only married to a German. He had only followed your mother for a short time to Germany . . .

TEMPLAR: Enough! Please! What about Recha's brother? Recha's brother . . .

NATHAN: You're her brother!

TEMPLAR: I am? I'm her brother?

RECHA: He's my brother?

SITTAH: Brother and sister!

SALADIN: They're brother and sister!

RECHA: [*Approaching him.*] Oh! My brother!

TEMPLAR: [*Stepping back.*] Her brother!

RECHA: [*Stops and turns toward Nathan.*] It can't be! Can't be! His heart knows nothing of this! We're impostors! God!

SALADIN: [*To the Templar.*] Impostors? What? Do you think so? Can you think so? You're the impostor! Everything about you is a lie: face and voice and walk! Nothing is yours! To refuse to recognize such a sister! Go!

TEMPLAR: [*Humbly coming nearer to him.*] Don't misunderstand my surprise, Sultan! Don't undervalue in a single moment, in which you scarcely saw your Assad, both him and me! [*Hurrying to Nathan.*] Nathan, you've taken from and given to me with full hands! No! You've given me more than you've taken from me! Infinitely more! [*Throwing his arms around Recha's shoulders.*] Oh! My sister! My sister!

NATHAN: Blanda von Filnek.

TEMPLAR: Blanda? Blanda? Not Recha? Not your Recha anymore? God! You're disowning her! You're giving her back her Christian name! You're disowning her on my account! Nathan! Nathan! Why are you making her pay for this? Her?

NATHAN: What do you mean? Oh, my children! My children! Don't you think my daughter's brother would be my child, as long as he wanted to be?

[*While they give themselves over to hugging each other, Saladin walks with uneasy astonishment toward his sister.*]

SALADIN: What do you say, sister?

SITTAH: I'm touched . . .

SALADIN: And I'm, I'm nearly recoiling before a greater emotion! Just prepare yourself for it as well as you can.

SITTAH: What?

SALADIN: Nathan, just a word! A word!

[*While Nathan steps over to him, Sittah steps over to the brother and sister to share the moment with them; Nathan and Saladin speak more softly.*]

SALADIN: Listen, just listen, Nathan! Didn't you just say . . .

NATHAN: What?

SALADIN: Her father wasn't from Germany, wasn't a German by birth. What was he then? Where did he come from?

NATHAN: He never wanted to tell. From his mouth I know nothing about it.

SALADIN: And so he wasn't another kind of Frank? Not a European?

NATHAN: Oh! He wasn't. He admitted that much. He preferred to speak Persian.

SALADIN: Persian? Persian? What more do I want? It's him! It was him!

NATHAN: Who?

SALADIN: My brother! Quite certainly! My Assad! Quite certainly!

NATHAN: Well, if you think that yourself, verify it in this book! [*Handing him the breviary.*]

SALADIN: [*Eagerly opening it.*] Ah! His handwriting! I recognize that too!

NATHAN: They still don't know anything of this! It's up to you alone how much they know of it.

SALADIN: [*Flipping through the book.*] Me, not recognize my brother's children? My niece and nephew—my children? Not recognize them? Me? Leave them to you? [*Aloud again.*] It's them! It's them, Sittah! Them! It's them! They're both my . . . your brother's children! [*He runs to join them in their hugs.*]

SITTAH: [*Following him.*] What am I hearing? How could it possibly be otherwise?

SALADIN: [*To the Templar.*] Now you have to love me, you have to, you stubborn boy! [*To Recha.*] Now am I not what I asked your permission to be? Whether you like it or not!

SITTAH: So am I! So am I!

SALADIN: [*To the Templar again.*] My son! My Assad! My Assad's son!

TEMPLAR: I'm from your blood! So those bedtime stories they used to tell me were more than stories! [*Falling to his feet.*]

SALADIN: [*Lifting him up.*] Look at this scoundrel! He knew something of this, and nearly made me his murderer! Just you wait!

[*The curtain falls to silent, repeated hugs from all sides.*]

PART THREE

Related Documents

1

JOHANN ANDREA EISENMENGER

Jewry Revealed

1711

Johann Andrea Eisenmenger (1654–1704) was a professor at the University of Heidelberg who spent much of his career defaming Judaism and the Jews. The excerpt below comes from his book Entdecktes Judenthum *[Jewry Revealed], one of the most virulently anti-Jewish attacks of all time. First published in Frankfurt in 1700, the book was suppressed by the authorities, who feared that it would incite violence against the local Jewish community. Yet it reappeared in Berlin in 1711 and came out in other editions later in the eighteenth century. Most of the book condemns the Talmud, or post-biblical "Oral Law," which Jews considered as sacred as the books of the Old Testament, and which according to Eisenmenger advocated immoral and even criminal behavior in relations with Christians. Worse still, Eisenmenger repeated the medieval accusations of ritual murder that had long been leveled against the Jews. He depicted them as sadistic murderers who took pleasure in torturing and killing Christians, including children, and who engaged in such monstrous activities out of the conviction that their religion commanded them to do so. His accusations are absurd, and no serious historian would give them the slightest credence. In his own day, however, and throughout Lessing's lifetime, many people believed Eisenmenger's accounts. The fact that the author was a respected professor lent credibility to his claims, and his practice of citing a publication for each accusation gave an aura of truthfulness to his libels, though his "sources" were equally preposterous and merely show the extent to which Gentiles were prepared to believe the worst about Jews. The following excerpt from this deeply disturbing book, although it has not the slightest value as a work of history, shows how unexpected Lessing's positive depiction of a Jewish character would have been to contemporaries who thought like Eisenmenger.*

Excerpted from Johann Andrea Eisenmenger, *Entdecktes Judenthum* (Königsberg, 1711), vol. 2, 218–25.

[T]he Godless Jews have no scruples about killing a Christian, and have done so not only to many old Christians, but also frequently and godlessly to young, innocent children, out of pure, bitter hatred against Christians, as is attested to sufficiently by the historians from whom I wish to draw here. Socrates[1] reports in his Church history, in the seventh book, in the thirteenth chapter, that in the Year of Christ 418 the Jews of Alexandria banded together, wore rings of woven palm bark around their fingers as signs, and afterwards screamed that the Christian church known as the Alexander Church was on fire. But when the Christians rushed there to put out the supposed fire, the Jews lay in wait for them and murdered as many as they could. For this reason the Bishop Cyril expelled all the Jews from Alexandria the next day.

In the Year of Christ 1321 the Jews in France poisoned the wells . . . resulting in the death of many people, and all of the guilty parties were burned on the order of King Philip, as reported in Heinrich Anselm von Ziegler's daily *Schauplatz,* year 1695, printed in Frankfurt in folio, page 5, column 2, and Sebastian Münster's *Cosmographia,* printed in Basel in the year 1550, page 192, in the second book. They did the same thing in the year 1348 in Switzerland and Alsace, as one can read in the Münster *Cosmographia,* pages 656 and 660, and Ziegler's *Schauplatz,* page 353, columns 1 and 2, as well as in *Cluverii Epitome historiarum,* printed in Breslau in the year 1672, page 577, column 2. And such deeds as Ziegler reports were known to the Jews and discussed among them. They had concluded from the dissension between the Emperor and the Pope that the downfall of the Christians was at hand, and wished to further this process with poison. But they received their well-earned reward, as many of them were burned in Basel, Strasbourg and Mainz. In other places they were stuffed into the same poison bags that were found in the wells and thus thrown into the water and drowned, though others were stabbed to death, thrown from their houses and otherwise, regardless of their age or sex, executed by every conceivable means of killing. The Jesuit Mattaeus Raderus reports such well-poisoning by Jews in his *Bavaria sancta,* in the second part, page 315: and in the third part, which was printed in Munich in the year 1627, he writes on pages 172, 173 and 174 that [the Jews] themselves admitted [to the poisonings].

In the Year of Christ 1349 the Jews of Meiningen, a city in Franconia, wanted to attack and kill the Christians while they were in church, but a girl heard and discovered these plans at the Jews' synagogue, so

---

[1]*Not* the Greek philosopher. [Ed.]

the Christians all went out of their church, took their weapons and killed all the Jews, as one finds in the [above-]mentioned *Schauplatz* of Ziegler, page 396, columns 1 and 2.

In the year 1571 Joachim II, Elector of Brandenburg, of most blessed Christian memory, was poisoned by a Jew with whom he had been very close, as Schleidanus reports in the tenth book of his *Historien,* page 60. In the same year M. A. Bragadinus was skinned alive by the Jews and cruelly murdered, as Sebastian Münster shows in his *Cosmographia.* And Cluverius reports in his *Epitome historiarum,* page 386, column 1, that when the Persian King Cosroes captured the city of Jerusalem in the Year of Christ 1611, at the time of Emperor Eraclius, and killed very many Christians, the Jews paid the ransom of ninety thousand Christian prisoners at a low price, and killed them all in a miserable manner.

On May 12 in the year 1665 in Vienna, in the Jewish quarter, a woman was cruelly murdered by the Jews, and was found in a pool in which horses were watered, in a sack on which a fifty-pound stone was hanging, and the body was wounded with many stabs, but the head and both shoulders, together with the legs up to the knee, were cut off, as one reads in the [above-]mentioned Ziegler's *Schauplatz,* page 553, columns 1 and 2. Meanwhile comparable murders, together with theft and other vices were practiced by these same Jews, thus his Imperial Majesty[2] was moved by a most praiseworthy Christian zeal to decree the expulsion of the wicked Jews, and in the year 1670, on February 4, on the principal squares of Vienna, with public fanfare it would be announced that all Jews must leave there forever, and that by the evening of Corpus Christi no more should be seen: upon which more than 1400 Jewish persons left and moved in part to Turkey but in part to Venice, as one can find in the *Schauplatz,* page 99, column 1.

Concerning the tender, innocent little children who were horribly killed by the Jews there is much to write.

In the Year of Christ 419 in Syria, in a place called Inmestar, between Chalcyde and Antioch, the Jews were gambling and, after having become drunk on wine, began to insult not only the Christians, but even Christ. Afterwards they captured a Christian boy, bound him to a cross, hung him high on it, taunted him with laughs and finally killed him with blows, for which they nevertheless received their just reward, as one can read in the previously cited Church history of Socrates, in the seventh book, in the 16th chapter.

[2]Leopold I of Austria. [Ed.]

In the Year of Christ 1250 the Jews of Aragon also stole a seven-year-old boy, crucified him on their Easter,[3] stabbed him in the chest with a pike, and thus killed him, as is reported in Johannes à Lent's little book, *De Pseudo-Messis,* that is, "of the false Messiah," page 33, from the Aragonese chronicle of the same year. Cluverius also writes in his *Epitome historiarum,* page 541, column 1, that the Jews of London in the Year of Christ 1257 similarly killed a Christian child for their annual sacrifice.

In the Year of Christ 1282 it happened in Munich that a woman who was a sorceress sold the Jews there a little boy, whom they stabbed all over his body and cruelly murdered; and when the same witch wanted to steal another boy and bring him to the same [Jews], she was caught by the child's father and accused, upon which, after undergoing torture, she admitted the deed and indicated the place where the murdered child had been placed, and she was thereafter executed. When the people of Munich saw the face of the child who had been stabbed to death, they were so embittered against the Jews that they beat all the Jews in that area to death, as can be seen with more information in Mattaeus Raderus's above-mentioned book, *Bavaria sancta,* in the second part, page 315, from the seventh book of *Aventini annalium Bojorum.*

In the Year of Christ 1303 a boy at Weissensee in Thuringia, and in the year 1305 one in Prague, were killed at Easter in the same cruel manner, as the highly learned Mr. Tentzel reports in his monthly discussion of July 1693, page 556. And in the year 1345 again a little boy in Munich, named Heinrich, was killed by the Jews there, who opened his veins and stabbed him sixty times, as the previously cited Raderus indicates in his [above-]mentioned book, *Bavaria sancta,* in the second part, page 333, in the seventh book of the *Aventini.*

In the Year of Christ 1475, on the evening of Holy Thursday, the Jews of Trent, through a Jew named Tobias, captured a poor Christian child named Simon who was not fully two and a half years old, and brought him to the house in which they had their synagogue, where they were all assembled. Then an old Jew named Moses took the child on his lap, undressed him, and stuck a handkerchief in his mouth, so that he could not scream, while the others held him by his hands and feet. Moses gave him a wound with a knife in his right cheek and cut out a piece of flesh. Those who were standing around collected the blood, and each cut out a little piece of flesh with scis-

---

[3]Eisenmenger is referring to the Jewish holiday of Passover. [Ed.]

sors, until the wound had become as large as an egg, which they also did in other parts of the body. After this they stretched out his hands and arms like a crucifix and pierced through the half-dead body with many needles, and at the same time said some sayings with the following content: *Let us kill him, just like Jesus the God of the Christians, who is nothing: and may all our enemies die like this.* Finally, when the child, after enduring torture that lasted an entire hour, gave up the ghost, they hid him among the wine barrels, and after a feared careful house search, threw him in the flowing water near the synagogue, as one can read in Münster's *Cosmographia,* page 342, and in the book by the highly learned Mr. Sigismund Hofmann, consistorial and city preacher in Celle, printed in the year 1699 in Celle, which is called *Das schwer zu bekehrende Juden-Hertz* [The difficult to convert Jewish heart], page 115. And this murder is described to the greatest humiliation of the Jews here in Frankfurt under the bridge tower, and these words stand there: *Anno 1475* on Holy Thursday, the little child Simon was killed by the Jews.

To be sure, the Amsterdam Jew Isaacus Viva, in the tractate that he wrote in the Latin against Jacob Geusius, which is called *Vindex Sanguinis,* tried to deny the murder that took place in Trent, by placing on page 17 . . . a certificate from the Chancellery of Padua in which it is reported that this matter was invented. But Mr. Tentzel meticulously maintains the contrary in his monthly discussion from July 1693, page 551, etc., and with unobjectionable reasons. He thus writes on pages 552 and 553 of the same work that the mayor of Trent, who is called Johannes della Salle, was ordered by the Inquisition to have a Christian from Trent, who had converted from Judaism several years earlier, to come to him. And he asked him what particular customs the Jews have at Easter. And [the Jew] answered that on the fourth day of Holy Week the Jews bake the unleavened bread and typically mix it with the blood of a Christian child, [and] mix this blood with their wine on the fifth and sixth days of their Easter, and in their customary meal prayer and blessing add a curse against the Christians, that God should send them all the plagues of the Egyptians and of Pharaoh. Supposing this is invented, there are so many other examples of child murder that the Jews have committed in many lands that they cannot be cleared of such bloodlettings, as has been shown in the preceding [pages], and as will be substantiated in what follows.

In the Year of Christ 1486 the Jews of Regensburg killed with their murderous hands six children, who were found in an underground cellar, and whose remains were brought to the local city hall. In the same cellar was found a large stone covered with lime, under which blood was found, since the children had been killed with the stone, as one can read in the *Raderi Bavaria sancta,* in the third part, page 172.

In the Year of Christ 1509 the Jews of Bosingen, a marketplace in Hungary, kidnapped a cartwright's little child, dragged him into a cellar, [and] most cruelly tortured him by cutting all his little veins and drawing his blood out with quill feathers. After that deed they threw the body into a thick thorn bush on the spot, where it was found by a woman, and the matter was referred to the authorities, who had the suspected Jews thrown into prison. Although they denied the deed, they finally admitted it under torture, as is reported in the often-cited daily *Schauplatz* of Ziegler, page 588, columns 1 and 2.

In the Year of Christ 1540, in a place in the Upper Palatinate, in the principality of Neuburg, which is called Sappenfeld and lies not far from Neuburg, a little boy named Michael, four and a half years old, whose father was called Georg Pisenharter, was taken away by the Jews before Easter and brought to Titingen. They bound him to a column, tortured him for three days, cut off his fingers and toes, cut crosses throughout his body and ripped him apart so badly that he could no longer be wounded. This murder came out through a young Jew, who had told other Jew-boys on the street that "the dog died after three days of howling," which was heard by the neighbors. [The Jews had] carried the body into the hedges in a forest and covered it with leaves, which a shepherd's dog found, upon which many people came together and saw how the child had been killed; and his blood was later found in Posingen, as the above-cited *Raderus* thoroughly shows in his book, *Bavaria sancta,* in the third part, page 176, etc.

In the Year of Christ 1598 in Poland a child was killed by the Jews, as is written in the monthly discussion of July 1693, page 557, by Papebroch, volume 2, . . . in which it is also reported that the child's blood was used in their unleavened bread and wine at the Easter festival, which a rabbi named Isaac admitted. Papebroch brings up twelve other examples of such murders, which all occurred in Poland.

In the Year of Christ 1650, on March 11, a Jew in Caaden mortally wounded a child with two major stabs and six other stabs and tears and cut the fingers off both his hands. But the Jew was taken into custody and on the 21st of March sentenced to death by breaking on the wheel, as one can see in the previously cited monthly discussions of January 1694, page 148, as well as in December 1694, page 975, from the book by the Jesuit Georgius Crugerius, which is called *Sacri pulveres.* It also says in the reported discussions of January 1694, page 152, that similar barbaric murders by the Jews of Steiermark,

Carinthia and Crain took place. Further one reads in the discussions of July 1693 by the above-mentioned Papebroch, volume 2, the 17th day of April, pages 504 and 505, many more examples collected of Christian children murdered by Jews in Germany, and is told the reasons of Bonfinius and Cantipratanus: because the Jews believed that Christian blood has the power to stop the bleeding of circumcisions, excites love, stops menstruation, etc., and that they use it in an old but secret prayer in order to appease God with a daily offering of Christian blood. Further in the discussions of July 1693, page 553, one can read that 40 years ago the Jews in Lower Germany slaughtered a Christian child at their Easter festival, upon which, when the matter became public, more than 45 of them were burned.

In the year 1669, on September 25, a Jew from Metz named Raphael Levi, on the open road near the town of Glatigny, took a child of 3 years from a resident of [Glatigny] named Gilles le Moyne, and brought him under his coat back to Metz on his horse, whereupon said Raphael Levi, after secluded testimony that he had stolen [the child], was taken into custody and after much discussion of the matter was burned alive on January 17, 1670. But the child's little head was found with a part of his neck, and some ribs, together with some of his clothes and a red cap, in the forest near Glatigny, and had been carried there by a Jew named Gedeon Levi who lived in the town of Hez, all of which one can see in the sixteenth part of a little paper-bound book called *Abbregé du procés fait aux Juifs de Mets,* that is, *Short Contents of the Trial Held Against the Jews of Metz,* which was lent to me by a good friend just as I was writing this material, [and] in which the whole matter is meticulously described.

More about such revolting and monstrous Jewish murders can be read in the above-mentioned book, *Das schwer zu bekehrende Juden-Hertz;* also Genebrardus in the fourth book, page 343, etc., and the book *Fortalitium fidei,* in the third book can be consulted. But one hears no more of such cruel deeds at the present time in Germany, except for one that I, if I remember correctly, read about some years ago in the newspaper, in which a murdered child was found in Franconia and the Jews were therefore held in suspicion. For since the Jews are dealt with severely wherever such things are perpetrated, it is undoubtable that they now refrain from such bloodletting out of fear of punishment, although their hatred against the Christians is just as great as it has ever been. But it is clear to see from all that has been said above that the Jews have no scruples about killing a Christian, and that they must be allowed to [by their religion], as long as they can do so conveniently and secretly, without danger.

2

CHRISTIAN WILHELM VON DOHM

On the Civic Improvement of the Jews

1781

Not every non-Jew in Germany was as hostile toward the Jews as Eisen-menger was, and Lessing was not the only Gentile who believed in the Jews' humanity. Christian Wilhelm von Dohm (1751–1820) was a Prussian official who sought to improve the legal conditions of the Jews in Germany. His treatise, Über die bürgerliche Verbesserung der Juden *[On the civic improvement of the Jews] (Berlin, 1781), argued for the abolition of laws that discriminated against the Jews and called for greater equality. At the same time, his book reveals his own prejudices, and although Dohm argued that historical circumstances rather than the Jews' religion or innate character were responsible for their vices, he did see them as less virtuous in general than their Christian neighbors. Thus the program of* Verbesserung *("improvement") was a call for the Jews' moral improvement as well as the amelioration of their legal condition.*

In almost all parts of Europe the laws and even the entire constitution of states aim to prevent as much as possible the increase in the number of those unhappy Asiatic refugees, the *Jews*. In some states they have been refused residence entirely, and travelers can only obtain, for a certain price, the protection of a territorial lord to stay for a short time (often only one night). Yet in most of the other states the Jews have only been accepted under the most burdensome conditions, and not even as citizens, but as simple inhabitants and subjects. At most a restricted number of Jewish families is allowed to settle in a territory, and this permission is typically restricted to specific locations and must be purchased with a considerable sum of money. In very many territories an already established fortune is the necessary condition for an authorized presence. If a Jewish father has many sons, he must transmit the privilege of living in the land of his birth to one of these;

Excerpted from Christian Wilhelm von Dohm, *Über die bürgerliche Verbesserung der Juden* [On the civic improvement of the Jews] (Berlin, 1781), 8–11, 14–18, 21–28, 34–39, 86–87, 109–12, 114–15, 118, 120–25.

he must send the others, along with a torn-off portion of his fortune, to foreign parts, where they will have to struggle with similar obstacles. With respect to his daughters he may or may not be lucky enough to establish them in one of the few families of his locality. Thus rarely can a Jewish father enjoy the happiness of living among his children and grandchildren, and of establishing the welfare of his family in a lasting manner. For even the wealthy one will be forced by the necessary costs of establishments in various places substantially to tear his fortune to pieces. Should the Jew be granted permission to reside in the state, he must repurchase this every year through a heavy tax; he cannot marry without special permission, which in turn depends on specific conditions and is not without additional costs; each child increases the size of his taxes, and almost all of his business affairs are laden with these. In every business of life the laws are ranged against him with the greatest severity, and the more lenient treatment of the other people among whom he lives makes his own all the harder to bear. And with so many taxes the Jew's productivity is most restricted. He is completely excluded from the honor of serving the state in peace as well as war; the greatest of occupations, farming, is everywhere forbidden to him, and almost nowhere can he possess landed property in his own name. Every guild would consider itself dishonored if it accepted one of the circumcised among its members, and the Hebrew is thus completely excluded from the crafts and the mechanical arts in almost every country. Only rare geniuses (who, when one speaks of the nation as a whole, cannot be counted on) possess sufficient courage and happiness under so many oppressive circumstances to raise themselves up to the fine arts and the sciences, of which, when viewed as a path to livelihood, only surveying, natural science and medicine remain to the Hebrew. And even those rare people who reach a high level in the sciences and arts, as well as those who honor themselves through irreproachable integrity, can only obtain the respect of a small number of nobles; for the majority of these even the most extraordinary accomplishments of the mind and the heart never excuse the error of being a *Jew*. This unhappy person, then, who has no Fatherland, whose occupations are everywhere hindered, who can never freely express his talents, whose virtue is not believed, for whom there is hardly any honor: to him there remains no other way of enjoying that existence which is permitted to him, and of nourishing himself, than *commerce*. But even this is impeded by many restrictions and taxes, and only a few among this nation have enough of a fortune to undertake wholesale commerce. They are therefore mostly restricted to very small retail commerce, in which only the frequent repetition of small profits can suffice to maintain a meager existence; or they are forced to lend their money, which they cannot use themselves, to others.

. . .

What grounds can the governments of the European states have for nearly unanimously imposing these harsh conditions on the Jewish nation? What has induced the aforesaid (and even the wisest among them) to make an exception of the Jews alone from all the laws of inspired politics, according to which all citizens must be induced through uniform justice, facility of sustenance, and the greatest possible freedom of action, to contribute to the good of the whole? Should many diligent and good citizens be less useful to the state because they are descended from Asia, because they distinguish themselves by beards, circumcision and a special way, passed down from their remotest forefathers, of worshipping the *Supreme Being*? This last characteristic [i.e., their religion] would certainly make them incapable of enjoying the equal rights with other citizens of the state, it would justify all of the restrictive measures, if it contained fundamental principles that prevented the Jews from fulfilling their duties toward the state, from being faithful and trustworthy in their actions toward civil society and its individual members; if it made it a duty to hate those who do not belong to their religion and authorized deception and the breaking of foreign laws.

It must be clearly proved that the religion of the Jews contains such unsociable principles, that its divine commandments stand in contradiction with the commandments of justice and philanthropy, if one wishes to justify before the eyes of reason completely denying the Jews the *rights of citizen* and only allowing them to enjoy incompletely those of man. So far as the Jewish religion has become known to us, it does not contain these harmful principles. Only the mob, which itself considers it permissible to cheat a Jew, accuses him of having the right, according to his law, to cheat members of other religions, and only persecuting priests have collected fables from the prejudices that support their own.[1]

---

[1]No writer has made more of an effort in collecting these fables, and none has done so with more spite and with a greater intention of intensifying and justifying the un-Christian and impolitic spirit of persecution, than Eisenmenger in his *Entdecktes Judenthum*. According to him there is no absurdity that is not believed by Jews, no prejudice that they are not nourished with, no vice that is not committed by them. One need only leaf through this book to be convinced that the evidence of his accusations consists

. . .

It is quite natural that the feelings of oppression under which the Jews of our day live should mix with the hostile attitudes that their holy law long ago fostered in their ancestors against the peoples whose land they were supposed to conquer, and perhaps some of them consider it permissible to hate as Canaanites people who hardly allow their existence in their societies. These attitudes, however, are indisputably nothing but inferences from their ancient law which feelings of oppression and contempt appear to justify. Yet it is certain that the current religion of the Jews contains no command of hatred or contempt for adherents of other religions. Murder, theft, deception, all remain crimes according to their law.[2] Still, conclusions of the type mentioned above can be and indeed are inferred by all religions. Each religion boasts of being the only, or at least the surest and most direct, path to the good will of the Divinity, to the enjoyment of the bliss of an afterlife; each considers its truth established by such clear, irrefutable proofs that only deliberate blindness could close one's eyes to lights which to it shine like the light of the sun. Each religion therefore drives into its adherents a kind of aversion toward those of all the others, an aversion that can border more or less on hatred and contempt, and which appears to be strengthened or weakened in many gradations, depending on how the political relations of the various religious

---

primarily of the testimony of converted Jews, who through such testimony about their former coreligionists sought to make themselves popular with their new coreligionists; [converted Jews] who were so ignorant that they knew as little about the religion that they abjured as that to which they converted, and who were normally disrespectful to both religions, and at least could not be cited as credible witnesses. The sometimes absurd and immoral opinions of specific rabbis can so little be used as proof against the whole Jewish teaching as the similar opinions of many Christian theologians can be counted against the holy teaching of the Gospel. [Dohm's note]

[2] One might find places in the Talmud where individual rabbis have endeavored to prove through sophistic induction that it is not such a great crime to deceive a person who does not belong to the Israelite people. Of this type is, e.g., the explanation of the law, "love your neighbor, do not insult him, etc.": "by 'neighbor' is meant only the Israelite." Some authors who are inimical to the Jews, and particularly Eisenmenger, have with these passages gathered many accusations against the Jewish nation and wished thereby to justify hatred and persecution of it. But if (as is indisputable) these opinions of specific teachers are never accepted by the [Jewish] nation; if neither the Mosaic law nor the Talmud and their greatest teachers have recognized any distinction between vice and crime, no matter whom they are committed against; then it would be unjust to attribute the prejudices of particular rabbis to the entire nation; precisely as unjust as it would be to judge the Christian religion according to the opinions of many Church Fathers (which are often enough irrational and misanthropic), and to try on this basis to derive the moral principles of Christians today. [Dohm's note]

societies affect their sensitivities with respect to each other, and on whether the rest of the culture, the influence of philosophy and the sciences, have left the impressions of the hallowed opinions weaker or stronger. If therefore every religion more or less tears the natural bonds of humanity, and does not grant the feelings and rights of humanity in equal measure to those who are divided by differing opinions, if this is a natural consequence of the presumed characteristics of every religion, then it cannot therefore count as a reason for denying the rights of citizens to the adherents of any particular religion. For otherwise the state would have to tolerate no religion or only one. Both options are in the current situation unfeasible, both would contradict the true interest of the state and would constitute an infringement on the natural rights of the human being, which all reserve in their capacity as citizens, and among which especially is the freedom to search for the surest path, according to one's opinion, to the happiness of an afterlife, and to worship the *Supreme Being* in the manner that one considers most worthy and appropriate. The diversity of principles and the resulting divisions are a natural and inevitable consequence of this freedom, but this diversity, when viewed and treated from the proper perspective, is not as disadvantageous for the state as often believed. This division accomplished by religion is not the only one in civil society. All members of the latter are united in manifold relationships in various isolated associations and specific little societies; each of these has its own peculiar principles, inculcates in its members its own attitudes and prejudices, and gives them . . . special motives for activity and education. Each of these associations attributes to itself superior characteristics and distinguishes itself from other human beings in a more or less disadvantageous way. Thus are divided noble, burgher and peasant; city-dweller and rural inhabitant; soldier and civilian; scholar and layman; artist and the uninitiated. Thus is separated one guild, one craft, one business in the state, and all its members, from all the rest, and thus are separated Christian, Jew and Muslim, the followers of Ali and Osman, the venerators of the Pope and of Luther, of Socinus and Calvin, the Portuguese and Polish Hebrews.[3]

---

[3]"The followers of Ali and Osman" are, respectively, Shi'ite and Sunni Muslims. The Shi'ite Muslims believe that Ali, Muhammad's son-in-law, was his only legitimate successor, whereas the Sunnis hold to a longer line of successors or *Caliphs*. The reference to Osman comes from the fact that the thirteenth-century Turkish leader Osman (whose name is preserved in the later "Osman" or Ottoman Empire) was a strong supporter of the Sunni branch of Islam. The Pope is the head of the Roman Catholic Church. Martin

The great and noble business of the government is to mitigate the exclusive principles of all these various societies so that they are not disadvantageous to the large association that embraces them all, so that each of these divisions only stimulates competition and skill and does not give rise to aversion and separation, and that these divisions all dissolve in the great harmony of the state. Let the government allow each of these special associations its pride, even those prejudices that are not harmful; but let it endeavor to inspire in each member even more love for the state, and it will have reached its great goal when the noble, the peasant, the scholar, the artisan, the Christian and the Jew are more *citizens* than they are any of the aforesaid. Thus in the great states of antiquity no belief in various gods divided the citizens, to whom the Fatherland was the dearest of all; and thus do Catholics, Episcopalians and Puritans now fight on the other side of the ocean for the new state that should unite them all, and for the freedom and rights that they all wish to enjoy.[4] And thus do we too already see in some of the European countries the citizens harmoniously united for the happiness of this life, even if they seek on various paths the happiness of the life to come. If therefore there were a few principles contained in the religions of today's Jews that would shut them too tightly in their particular association and cut them off too exclusively from the rest of the members of civil society; even this, as long as their commands do not contradict those of general morality, would not justify their persecution, which can only serve to attach them all the more strongly to their attitudes. The only task of the government here must be first to know exactly those principles, or much more, only those inferences from religious principles and their actual influence on practices. And then it must make an effort to weaken this influence by promoting the general enlightenment of the [Jewish] nation and morality independent from religion, and the refinement of

---

Luther (1453–1546) established Protestantism in opposition to the Pope. Faustus Socinus (1539–1603) was considered a heretic for his denial of the Trinity (the unity of the Father, Son, and Holy Spirit). John Calvin (1509–1564) created a split within Protestantism by emphasizing the doctrine of predestination, according to which everything is predetermined by God. The "Portuguese and Polish Hebrews" are the Sephardic and Ashkenazi Jews, respectively. Sephardic Jews descend from the Jews who were expelled from Spain and Portugal at the end of the fifteenth century, whereas Ashkenazi Jews have central European ancestors. Although the two groups did not differ fundamentally in matters of religion, in the eighteenth century they tended to live separately and to regard each other with suspicion. [Ed.]

[4]This is an allusion to the American Revolution. [Ed.]

their sentiments. Above all the taste of civic happiness in a well-ordered state and of the freedom so long refused would drive away all unsociable religious attitudes. The Jew is more a human being than a Jew, and how could he not love a state in which he can freely acquire property and freely enjoy it, where his taxes would not be higher than those of other citizens, and where he could also gain honor and respect? Why would he hate people who no longer distinguish themselves from him through offensive privileges, and with whom he has the same rights and duties? The novelty of this happiness, and, alas, the probability that he will not be allowed it soon in all states, would make it all the more precious to the Jew, and gratitude would necessarily make him into a patriotic citizen. He would regard the Fatherland with the tenderness of a once disowned son who only after a long exile is restored in his filial rights. These human feelings would speak more loudly in his heart than all the sophistic deductions of his rabbis.

. . .

I can admit that the Jews may be more morally corrupt than other nations; that they make themselves guilty of petty crimes in relatively greater numbers than the Christians; that their character on the whole may be more inclined toward usury and deception in business, their religious prejudices may be more divisive and asocial; but I must add that this presumed greater corruption of the Jews is a necessary and natural consequence of the oppressive constitution under which they have found themselves for so many centuries. A calm and impartial consideration will not leave the truth of this supposition in doubt.

The hard and oppressive condition in which the Jews live almost everywhere would even explain a much greater degree of corruption than that of which one can in truth accuse them. Quite naturally the Jew's soul will, as a result of this condition, grow unaccustomed to noble feelings, sink into the base business of worrisome daily sustenance. The many forms of oppression and contempt that he experiences must naturally quash his activities and suffocate every feeling of honor in his heart. Since he is left almost no honest means of nourishing himself, it is natural that he should sink into cheating and fraud, into which commerce, more than other types of livelihood, tends to tempt one. How can one be surprised that the Jew only believes himself bound to the laws, which barely allow him an existence, when he cannot violate them with impunity? How can one demand of him willing obedience and love of the state in which he sees himself tolerated only insofar as he is able to pay taxes? How can one be surprised at his hatred for a nation that gives so many perceptible proofs of its hatred for his? How can one expect virtue from him if no one believes him capable of it? How can one accuse him of infractions that one forces him to commit, since he is allowed no innocent livelihood, is oppressed by taxes and has nothing left with which he could provide himself with the fostering and moral education of his virtue?

Everything of which the Jews are accused is caused by the political constitution in which they now live, and any other kind of human being, placed in the same circumstances, would make himself guilty of the same petty crimes. For those corresponding peculiarities of thinking, temperament and passions which are found in the greater part of individual members of a nation, and which one calls their *particular character,* are not decisive and immutable features of their own modification of human nature; rather, as has been clearly recognized in our day, they are the result partly of climate, nutrition, etc., even more importantly of the political constitution in which a nation is located.[5] If then the Jew in Asia is different from the Jew in Germany, this will have to be seen as the consequence of the differing physical situations; but if the Jew in Cracow and the Jew in Cadiz are both accused of deception in business, etc., this must be the result of the same oppression that Jews experience all the way to the far ends of Europe. The accusation that today's Jews abhor Christians with precisely the same fanatical hatred with which their ancestors crucified Christ hardly deserves a serious response. Only in the ages of barbarism could the distant descendants in France and Germany be held accountable for a crime that was committed many centuries earlier on the Asian coast of the Mediterranean sea. Truly the unsociable mutual aversion of the two religious societies, which have a common origin, remains stronger after such a long period of time and despite such progressive enlightenment than the philosopher would expect or wish. But precisely this is the fault of governments that have not been wise enough to mitigate the divisive religious principles, and have not been able to stimulate in the *heart of Jews and of Christians* a *civic feeling* that would necessarily have consumed the prejudices of both long ago. These governments were Christian, and we therefore, if we wish to remain impartial, cannot deny the accusation that *we* have contributed the most to the unsociable temperament of both parties. We were always the rulers, it was therefore up to us to instill human feelings in

[5]Dohm is referring to the theory of the French political philosopher Montesquieu (1689–1755), as laid out particularly in *De l'esprit des lois* [Of the spirit of the laws] (1755). [Ed.]

the Jew by giving him proof of our own; we must, in order to cure him of his prejudices against us, first give up our own. If it is then these prejudices that still prevent the *Jew* from being a good *citizen,* a sociable human being, if he feels aversion against and hatred toward the Christian, if he does not believe himself bound to the laws of integrity; this is *all our work.* His religion does not command him these infractions, but the prejudices that we have instilled in him and still remain with him, have a stronger effect than religion. We are guilty of the infractions with which we charge him; and the moral corruption in which this unhappy nation is mired, due to our mistaken policies, cannot be a reason justifying the perpetuation of these policies.

[After describing the persecutions of Jews from Roman times to his own day, Dohm continues:]

These principles which, in contradiction to both humanity and good government, still bear so clearly the stamp of the dark centuries in which they originated, are unworthy of the Enlightenment of our times and have long since ceased to deserve being followed. Our well established states must be welcome to every citizen who obeys the laws and increases the state's wealth through his diligence; they must not, as did those dominions of crude nations established by force, with simultaneous barbarism and fear, banish or oppress foreigners. No one in [the well established states] is unworthy of the rights of citizen, except the criminal and the one who permits himself unsociable transgressions or counsels persecution. The most differing principles concerning the life to come do not prevent the unity of attitudes regarding one's duties in this life vis-à-vis the state or the fulfillment of those duties. The enjoyment of the freedom to follow one's own particular opinions with regard to [religious principles] endears the citizens more to the state that allows this freedom, and at the same time dulls all arrows of fanaticism. With the greatest diversity of religious societies, the prejudices of each is least worrisome to the state; and it will be most difficult for the hallowed teachings to instill exclusive principles in their worshippers when the state embraces all with equally impartial love, when they can completely enjoy the advantages of civil society without offending the belief of their fathers.

The Jew as well has a claim to this enjoyment, to this love. His religion does not make him unworthy of these, since he can, in strictest observance of it, be a very good citizen. If the oppression under which he has lived for centuries has made him more morally corrupt [than

Christians], just treatment will make him better again. It is possible that some faults are so deeply rooted that they will only begin to disappear in the third or fourth generation. But this is no reason not to begin reform immediately, since without it the improved generation would never appear.

. . .

I now dare . . . to state more precisely my ideas on how the Jews can become happier and better members of civil society.

In order to make them so, they must *first* enjoy the same rights as all other subjects. They are capable of fulfilling the requisite duties, and can therefore rightfully claim immediately the state's impartial love and care. No insulting distinctions may be further tolerated, no means of livelihood closed to them. . . . All the usual state taxes must be collected from them as well, but their mere existence must not be purchased with protection money, and the right to nourish themselves must not be paid for. . . .

Second. Since it is the restriction of Jews' employment to commerce that has given their moral and political character a disadvantageous direction, the complete freedom of employment and means of livelihood are appropriate equally for justice and for the philanthropic policy of forming the Jews into useful and happy members of society. It might even be advisable, toward the accomplishment of this great goal, for the government first to divert the Jews from the occupation of commerce and to try to weaken its influence by giving them more opportunities and incentives to practice the kind of occupation that is most capable of influencing a refractory spirit and attitudes; I mean the handicrafts. The sedentary lifestyle and calm diligence that these promote is opposed to the restless wandering of the trading Jew, as are the [artisan's] calm enjoyment of the present and satisfaction with little opposed to [the Jew's] hopes for the future, his greed for profit, his calculations of ever fluctuating percentages. At the same time the hard work and the artisan's coarser and stronger diet will have an advantageous influence on his physical constitution; the mechanical skills will develop new abilities; work that is always the same and a middling standard of living will make the Hebrew more like the orderly citizen and inhabitant of the cities. . . .

Third. Nor should the Jews be prohibited from agriculture. If the acquisition of landed property in a territory has not been restricted to specific classes of inhabitants, then the Jews must not be prevented from otherwise enjoying fully equal rights, at least by means of leasing. Nevertheless I would not expect very considerable advantages from the keeping of large estates, since this business . . . has too much in common with commerce and too greatly nourishes the spirit of speculation and profit. I would not like to see the Jews encouraged to become large landowners or lease-holders (which in any case only few have the means to become), but rather true farmers who actually work their own land. The money that in many states is now spent on colonists would in many cases be better allocated if it were remitted toward native industrious Jews for small, untilled plots of land and residences and thus supported them in their initial agricultural expenses. It might even be permissible to reanimate the spirit of this occupation in the [Jewish] nation by requiring Jewish lease-holders or owners of large estates to work the land with a certain number of Jewish farm workers. . . .

Fifth. Every art, every science, must be open to the Jew as well as to every other free person. He too must educate his mind, as far as he can, and his developed talents should lead him to distinction, honor and reward. The scientific establishments must be open to the Jew as well, and there must be no more limitations to the means of applying his skills than there is to any other member of society. . . .

Sixth. It must be a special goal of a wise government to care for the Jews' moral education and enlightenment, and thereby to make coming generations at least susceptible to mild treatment and the enjoyment of all the advantages of society. Of course the state should not concern itself with their religious instruction unless it is necessary to prevent the propagation of unsociable attitudes against those who think differently. But it can see to it that the Jews' minds are enlightened by the bright light of reason, by knowledge of nature and its great Author, and that their hearts are warmed by the principles of order, justice, and love of all humanity and the great society in which they live; it can see to it that the Jew too is led early to the sciences that his future occupation more or less demands. This should take place in the Jewish schools or, if in these teachers and funds should be lacking, the Jews should be allowed to send their children to Christian schools (except during the hours devoted to religious instruction). . . .

Seventh. Yet with the moral improvement of the Jews the effort of Christians to rein in their prejudices and hard-hearted attitudes must proceed at the same pace. Early in their youth Christians must already be taught to see the Jews as their brothers and fellow human beings who have chosen another path to obtain God's pleasure; a path that they no doubt erroneously believe to be the right one, but about which, if they follow it with the righteousness of their hearts, as God himself permits, people should not quarrel, but [Christians] should, on the contrary, through love lead [the Jews] to the conviction of an even greater truth. Preachers must be instructed to repeat often these principles, so appropriate to the spirit of philanthropy and respect for Christianity, to their congregations, and how easy it will be to follow this instruction when the spirit of love, which reigns in the *parable of the [good] Samaritan,* fills their heart, and when they, like the apostle of Christ, teach that *everyone of all nations who does good is pleasant to God. . . .*

Ninth. Both the written laws of Moses that are not related to Palestine or its former legal and religious constitution and those [laws] preserved through oral transmission, are kept by the Jews as the ever-binding commandments of God. Also the Jewish teachers' various explanations of and arguments relating to these laws maintain a legal status in the [Jewish] nation. If one therefore wishes to allow them the complete enjoyment of the rights of humanity, then it is necessary to allow them to live and be judged by these laws. They will in this respect be no more separated from the rest of the state's citizens than a state or community that lives according to special statutes; and the experience both in the earliest times of the Roman Empire and in many modern states has already taught that the *autonomy* authorized to the Jews gives rise to no unpleasant or disadvantageous consequences.

3

FRANÇOIS-LOUIS-CLAUDE MARIN

History of Saladin

1758

Just as prejudice against Jews was widespread in eighteenth-century Europe, so was prejudice against Muslims. Europeans typically depicted Muslims as ruthless, temperamental, and dogmatic, and although the

Excerpted from François-Louis-Claude Marin, *Histoire de Saladin, Sulthan d'Egypte et de Syrie* [History of Saladin, Sultan of Egypt and Syria] (The Hague, 1758), vol. 1, 309–12; vol. 2, 69–72, 200–201, 320–21, 325–30, 334–339.

Enlightenment was famous for advocating religious tolerance, its adher-
ents were quick to condemn religions they considered "fanatical." Thus
Islam, like Judaism, could equally become a target for traditional Chris-
tians or partisans of the Enlightenment. Moreover, political philosophers
viewed Muslim states as examples of despotism, that is, unlimited and
arbitrary rule. The following depiction of Saladin, written by François-
Louis-Claude Marin (1721–1809) is therefore remarkable for its positive
assessment of the Muslim ruler. For Marin, Saladin was unquestionably
an absolute ruler, but one who used his power for the good of his subjects.
To employ an expression that later commentators would use to describe
such a phenomenon, Marin considered Saladin an "enlightened despot."
By contrast, the Christian figures in this historical account, including the
Patriarch of Jerusalem, appear bloodthirsty, petty, and hypocritical. One
can see how this book must have appealed to Lessing, who in fact con-
sulted it when preparing his Nathan the Wise.

[Description of Eraclius, the Patriarch of Jerusalem:]

He was an Auvergnac[1] of bad morals and a pleasant appearance, a
poor man who, without resources in his homeland, like so many others came to try his luck in Syria. The Queen Mother[2] liked his looks,
to the disgrace of Christendom. She covered him with favors and soon
procured the Archbishopric of Caesarea[3] for him. The Patriarch of
Jerusalem having died in the meantime, two prelates claimed this
position: Eraclius and William, the Archbishop of Tyre.[4] The latter
was qualified by his services rendered to the state, his distinguished
accomplishments, a rare erudition and, still rarer in this perverse century, his virtue. But the Queen was not ashamed to solicit the patriar-
chate for her lover, nor was the clergy ashamed to choose him, nor
the King to confirm this election. William felt obliged to have this
unworthy concurrent deposed and filed a complaint with the Holy
See[5]. . . . Eraclius preserved through a crime what he had acquired by
crime. He had his rival poisoned. . . .

---

[1]A native of the Auvergne, a province in central France. [Ed.]
[2]Mary, the mother of [the Byzantine Emperor] Manuel Comnenus. [Marin's note]
[3]Caesarea was a Mediterranean port city in northern Palestine (today Israel). An
archbishopric was a principal administrative unit of the Catholic Church. [Ed.]
[4]A port city in southern Lebanon. [Ed.]
[5]The Vatican, the seat of the Catholic Church. [Ed.]

He returned in triumph to Syria, but when passing through Nablus[6] . . . he saw a certain Pasque de Riveri, unfortunately famed for her beauty and her debauchery. She was seduced by this man who sacrificed everything to his passions. Her husband, a modest local merchant, was an obstacle to this shameful business. This obstacle was quickly removed by a natural or violent death. Eraclius deservedly incurred the suspicion of having accelerated this poor man's days by poison. Be that as it may, he had his mistress brought to Jerusalem and did not blush to give her a palace, guards and high officers. The Queen herself did not have such magnificent clothes or such a sparkling entourage. This woman was only known as Madame the Patriarchess. She had in this rank a distinguished place in the Church. This was truly the abomination of desolation seated in the holy place. One day when the King had assembled the prelates and the barons of the kingdom to deliberate on an important matter, a man was seen entering the council and, all out of breath, shouting at Eraclius, "I've come to give you good news; Madame the Patriarchess, your wife, has just given birth."

[After Saladin has taken Jerusalem from the Crusaders, he threatens to kill the Christians to avenge the murder of Muslims by the Crusaders, but the Patriarch (not Eraclius but Balian) threatens to destroy Jerusalem and kill Muslim prisoners in the hands of Crusaders. After consulting his Imams and judges, Saladin decides that it is permissible to liberate the Christians on the payment of a ransom within forty days and to take the rest as slaves.]

But the poor who could not pay their ransom and would remain slaves according to the convention . . . let out the most horrible cries, tore out their hair in desperation and ripped their clothes. Meanwhile the fatal moment was approaching when they would have to leave the city; the term of forty days was about to expire.

Saladin was never so great as on this occasion, since true grandeur consists more in doing good for humanity through generous actions than in destroying it through murderous exploits and conquests. He sent guards and officers to all the quarters of the city, and sentries to every street, to suppress the violence of soldiers and to prevent them from insulting the Christians. He permitted the Greek

---

[6]A major city in Palestine. [Ed.]

and Syrian [Christians] to remain in Jerusalem and ceded the Church of the Holy Sepulchre to them. He wanted all the sick to be left at the hospitals, ordered that they be treated at his own expense, and permitted the Hospitaler brothers[7] to continue to receive care until their complete recovery.

At the same time the ransom was received from those who could pay. The poor were made slaves. The Sultan liberated a thousand at the request of his brother . . . and a thousand more at the solicitation of Balian.[8] . . . [He said], "Announce in the city that all the poor can leave and that I grant them their liberty." The historians inform us that the number was quite considerable. Finally the day came when it was necessary to empty the place. All the gates were closed, except that of David, through which the inhabitants were to file. Saladin, seated on his throne, had them pass by him, less to enjoy his victory and defy these unfortunates than to soothe their misery.

[. . .] Then one saw a large number of desolate women; they stretched their hands out to Saladin as suppliants and, in order to move him to compassion, showed him the little children for whom they were responsible, and shed a torrent of tears. Saladin asked them the reason for their affliction. "We have lost everything," they told him, "our houses, our property, our fatherland. We are about to wander without aid and without hope through a country that has become foreign to us. But, lord, you can ease our pain, if you are capable of pity. Return us our husbands, our fathers, our children whom you hold prisoner. They will serve us as guides on our route, they will sustain us in our weakness, and they will help us to bear our misfortunes." The Sultan, touched by their deplorable condition, sent for those among the captives of the previous battles that [the women] requested, and returned them. He did still more. He showered these women with gifts proportionate to their rank and their needs. Those whose relatives had perished in the war found reasons for consolation in his generosity. He gave them much more considerable gifts. No one came to him without receiving money or provisions. He gave these unhappy inhabitants more than he had gained [from conquest]. Finally an astonished Europe admired in a Muslim virtues unknown to the Christians of that century.

[7]The Hospitaler brothers, also known as the Hospitalers of St. John of Jerusalem or the Knights of Malta, specialized in medical care for sick or injured pilgrims. During the Crusades they were also fierce enemies of Islam; thus Saladin's clemency toward them is all the more remarkable. [Ed.]

[8]That is, Balian of Ibelin, the Patriarch of Jerusalem. [Ed.]

[More on Saladin's clemency:]

... the Sultan was presented with various prisoners of distinction, including a man who was overburdened by the weight of his years and could barely hold himself up. Saladin was moved at the sight of him; and after recuperating [the man's] strength by giving him food and drink, and dissipating his fear through signs of generosity, asked him through interpreters what country he was from. "My fatherland," he replied, "is so far away that it would take many months to reach it." "Then why, at your age," Saladin asked, "have you come so far to make war against me?" "I only undertook this voyage," the old man said, "in order to have the happiness of visiting the Holy Land before I die." "Then make your pilgrimage," Saladin added. "Be free, go and finish your days in the bosom of your family, and bring your children these signs of my benevolence." At the same time he gave him rich presents and a horse on which he was conducted to the Christian camp. He treated with no less regard the other captives, among whom the Arab [historians] say were the commandant of the French troops and the treasurer of the king of France. He spoke for a long time with them, lodged them in a tent near his, brought them often to his table, permitted them to send for all their things at camp, and allowed them to leave for Damascus.

[Marin relates a story about some of Saladin's sons:]

These princes asked their father's permission to cut off the heads of some Christian prisoners, believing that they would be committing a holy deed by killing enemies of their religion. "It does not please God," Saladin replied, "that I consent to such horrible cruelty. I do not want my children to grow accustomed to making a game of shedding human blood, whose value they do not know."

[Saladin's last words to his son El-Dhaher:]

Meanwhile Saladin sent his son El-Dhaher, who had returned to Jerusalem, to Upper Syria. Saying farewell to him, he said these remarkable words in the presence of Boha-eddin,[9] who recorded them: "My son, you are about to reign in the states that I have given you. My infirmities make me fear I will not see you again. I therefore recommend to

---

[9]Boha-eddin, alternatively spelled "Baha al-Din," was Saladin's biographer. [Ed.]

you, my son, as my last wish, to love, to honor God, who is the source
of all good, and to observe the precepts of his law, for your salvation
depends on it. Spare human blood, fear lest it fall back upon your
head. Shed blood never remains without an avenger. Strive to win the
heart and respect of your subjects; render them justice; take care of
their interests as your own. You will have to give an account to God
of this trust that I have bequeathed you in his name. Show respect
and consideration for the Emirs, the Imams, the Cadhis[10] and for all
persons here. It is only by mildness, moderation, clemency that I
have risen to the degree of elevation at which you see me. We are all
mortal, oh my son, therefore do not preserve any rancor, any hatred
against anyone. Above all take care not to offend any person. Men
only forget insults after having gotten revenge or obtained satisfaction,
despite the fact that God pardons our faults upon our simple penance,
for he is beneficent and merciful." After having given these wise instructions to his son, he embraced him, shedding tears of compassion,
and let him go.

*[The Sultan's last days in Damascus, his death and an assessment of his
character:]*

Meanwhile the rumor spread in the city [of Damascus] that the Sultan
was in danger. At this news the shops are closed; the markets are
emptied. Some go to prostrate themselves in the mosques, others run
to the palace: the gates are besieged; everyone leaving is stopped; the
doctors are questioned; one tries to read in their eyes whether there is
reason for hope or fear. The consternation of the Emirs passes into all
hearts: people cry, shriek, throw themselves toward the brink of
despair. The city is full of tumult and fear; no one recognizes distinctions anymore; the rich and the ordinary people, equally desolate,
mingle together, wander the streets, mix their sobs. The men spend
day and night at the gate of the palace; the women cry in the interior
of their houses; the priests address their prayers to Heaven. All feel
the pain of children about to lose a tenderly loved father; all would like
to give their lives to save that of their master.

During the few days that he still lived, Saladin was busy giving
instructions to his son Afdhal, who was to succeed him in the Kingdom of Damascus, and recommending that the Emirs help this prince

---

[10]Cadhis are Muslim judges who rule according to the Shari'ah, the religious law of
Islam.

and his other children with their wise counsel. He had alms distributed to all the poor, even to the indigent Christians who were in the city. As he had given everything during his life and had never saved anything for himself, it was necessary to sell his jewels and furniture. One of his sisters[11] responsible for this act of charity added her own belongings to make these alms more abundant. Contemporary historians say that the Sultan, before dying, ordered the officer who normally carried his standard in the army to attach at the top of a lance the sheet in which he was going to be buried and, while showing it to the people, to cry throughout the streets of Damascus, *Behold what Saladin, the Victor of the Orient, brings back from his conquests.*

Finally, on the twelfth day of his illness, Wednesday twenty-seven Sefer, second month of the Arabic year, the year five-hundred eighty-nine of the Hegira,[12] in the month of February, eleven hundred ninety-three of Jesus Christ, Saladin ended his career at the age of fifty-seven lunar years. He had reigned twenty-two years in Egypt since the death of the Caliph,[13] and nineteen in Syria, since the death of Noureddin. His full name was *Sultan, Malek al Nasser, Salah-eddin, emir el-Moumenin, Aboul Modhasser, Youssouf ben Ayoub, ben Schady;* that is to say, Sultan or Emperor, Defender King Salah-eddin, Preserver of the World and Religion, Commandant of the Faithful, Victorious Father, Joseph son of Job son of Schady.

It is easier to imagine than to describe the desolation of the inhabitants when they were told, *The Sultan is dead;* and when they saw several children of Saladin who were still at a very tender age suddenly leaving the palace, their clothes torn [in mourning], stretching their hands heavenward, imploring the pity of the people and traversing, moved by pain, the entire city, followed by citizens who could only respond with sobs. Boha-eddin, describing this sad spectacle and the effect it produced on the mind, observes that when he first heard that men were capable of devouring themselves for the sake of other men, he had taken this expression for a vain testimony of zeal, but that he then understood from the present condition of his soul and from the

[11]She was called Sittalscham or Sillah-Alscham. [Marin's note] She was the prototype for Sittah in *Nathan the Wise.* [Ed.]

[12]The Hegira was Muhammad's flight from Mecca to Medina in 622 C.E. and marks the beginning of the Muslim calendar. As it is a lunar calendar with either 354 or 355 days per year, 589 A.H. (Anno Hegirae, or "in the year of the Hegira") corresponds to 1193 C.E. [Ed.]

[13]Literally "successor" (i.e., to Muhammad), the Caliph was the chief Muslim leader, combining spiritual and political functions. [Ed.]

desperation of all the Muslims, that they would have willingly sacrificed their lives in return for that of the prince they had just lost. Mourning was universal throughout the empire, and even throughout the Orient. They prayed for Saladin in the mosques of Mecca and Medina,[14] an honor only accorded Caliphs and a few sovereigns who were most distinguished by their bravery, justice, humanity and piety.

Saladin was first buried in the palace, in the very apartment where he had fallen ill; but some time afterward, when Afdhal had a tomb erected near the mosque, his body was transported with pomp; and most of the Ajoubites[15] were present at this lugubrious ceremony.

If this Sultan carried the esteem and regrets of all the peoples, few princes deserved these sentiments for so many virtues. The Christians themselves could not prevent themselves from rendering him justice. It is they who have provided me with some of the characteristics spread throughout this history; I have been obliged to cut many of them that might appear minute to my readers.

Saladin observed so scrupulously the precepts of the Koran that the Muslims have placed him among their saints. He built mosques, schools and hospitals in all the principal cities; he took under his protection the elderly, the orphans, and nourished all who were indigent. There are those who claim he died a *philosophe;* he lived and died a religious man. It seems to some writers of our day that there cannot be truly great men without that philosophy which consists of not acknowledging any religion; at the same time they know that religion is a link that more strongly connects princes to their subjects than subjects to their princes; that breaking this link gives liberty to those men who can undertake anything with impunity; and that if there were no religion, it would perhaps be necessary for the good of humanity to fabricate one deliberately to put a powerful brake on the passions of sovereigns.

Saladin, far from disdaining the law of Muhammad, even adopted its most superstitious practices. This fault, which in the rest of humanity signals a weakness of the soul, in him was joined with much courage; for the idea of an irrevocable destiny regulating all the events of this world inspires intrepidity in every pious Muslim, especially in those wars undertaken for the glory of Islam. He exposed himself without fear to all dangers. Before battle he had the habit of riding his horse between the two armies, followed by a single horseman. During

---

[14]The holiest and second holiest city, respectively, in Islam. [Ed.]
[15]Members of Saladin's family. [Ed.]

the action he was the first in combat. Sometimes he advanced very close to the Franks, and then, stopping all of a sudden, he would have chapters of the Koran read to him while the Christians launched their arrows at him. Enemy of pageantry and indolence, he wore simple clothes, lived off little and nourished himself with ordinary food; his tent was the least magnificent of all. Hardened to fatigue, he rose before dawn, went riding every day, worked in the sieges like a simple soldier, presided over all attacks, ran the machines, was the first in any assault, and gave his troops the example of discipline, sobriety, faithfulness and courage that he wanted to inspire in them.

[Conclusions and final anecdotes:]

[Saladin's] clemency, his justice, his moderation, his generosity, much more than his conquests, have made his memory precious to all Muslims and to all those who know how to appreciate virtue. Few princes have taken such pleasure in giving. Master of Egypt, of Syria, of prosperous Arabia and of Mesopotamia, which paid tribute to him, he did not leave more than forty-seven drachmas of silver and a single *écu*[16] of gold in his coffers. It was necessary to borrow everything that was used for his funeral. He had neither a house, nor a garden, nor a city, nor land that belonged to him. Those of his children whom he had not provided with any government office, because of their youth, were reduced to serving their brothers or uncles for their subsistence. Saladin did not impose any new tax on his peoples; he reduced all and abolished many, despite the wars that he had to sustain during his reign. He gave cities and entire provinces as gifts. . . . At the siege of Ptolemais alone he gave his Emirs more than twelve thousand prize horses, not counting those of less value that he distributed to the soldiers. This is not an exaggeration, but a fact attested to by the officers of his stables. His excessive profusions [of generosity] resulted in his often lacking necessities. In addition, his treasurer had the habit of keeping some money without Saladin's knowledge, in case of pressing needs; but Saladin made this precaution useless by having his furniture sold when he had no more to give.

His justice was equal to his magnificence. He held his divan[17] himself every Monday and Thursday, together with his Cadhis, either in the city or the army. On the other days of the week he received

[16]A coin worth six pounds of silver. [Ed.]
[17]That is, council. [Ed.]

petitions, reports, requests and judged pressing cases. All persons without distinction of rank, age, nationality, religion found free access to him: Muslims, Christians, subjects, foreigners, the poor, the rich, all were admitted to his tribunal and judged according to the laws, or rather according to natural equity. . . . A certain Omar, merchant of Akhlat, a city independent of Saladin, even had the audacity to present a request against the monarch before the Cadhi of Jerusalem, demanding the return of a slave that the Sultan had sheltered. The astonished judge alerted Saladin to this man's pretensions and asked what ought to be done. *That which is just,* replied the Sultan. He appeared in court on the appointed day, defended his case by himself, and won; and far from punishing the temerity of this merchant, he had him given a large sum of money, wishing to compensate him for having had a high enough opinion of [Saladin's] integrity that he demanded justice in his own court, without fearing that it would be violated.

But his subjects often abused this facility; they importuned him at all hours of the day regarding their quarrels and private discussions. One day, after having worked all morning with his Emirs and his ministers, he removed himself from the crowd to take some rest. A slave came at that instant and requested an audience; Saladin asked him to return the next day. "My case," the slave responded, "cannot wait," and practically threw his request in his face. The Sultan picked up this piece of paper without becoming emotional, read it, found the request fair, and gave him what he solicited. Then, turning toward his officers who appeared surprised by such generosity, he said, *"This man has not offended me in the least: I have rendered him justice and done my duty."* Another time, while he was deliberating with his generals about the operations of the war, a woman presented him with a petition. Saladin had someone tell her to wait. *"And why,"* she cried, *"are you our king if you don't want to be our judge?"* *"She is right,"* the Sultan responded. He left the assembly, went up to this woman, listened to her complaints and sent her away satisfied.

Such was his clemency that he never punished any personal offense. This virtue often degenerated into a weakness and damaged the respect that was his due. We have seen in this history how easily he pardoned. Insults, outrageous words, sometimes overt disobedience, nothing made him lose his moderation. His soul was never troubled by any violent passion, never knew anger or vengeance, which is its consequence. Only religious zeal and the inhumanity of the Christians sometimes made him cruel towards them. His domestic servants stole from him; his treasurers embezzled his revenues without incurring any other penalty but removal from their positions. Once two Mamelukes were fighting a few steps away from him. One threw a shoe at the other; it missed its mark and hit the Sultan. But this prince pretended not to have noticed anything, turned a corner as if to speak with one of his generals, in order to avoid having to punish the perpetrator of this act. During the time when he was the most irritated against the Franks, due to the cruelty of Richard, and was having the heads cut off all those who were taken in combat, a Christian officer seized with mortal fear was pulled into his tent. When Saladin asked him the reason for his fear, the officer said, *"I was trembling when coming up to you; but I ceased to be afraid when I saw you. A prince whose face only displays goodness and clemency would not be so cruel as to condemn me to death."* The Sultan smiled and gave him his life and freedom.

We are forced to pass over in silence many similar anecdotes carefully reported by Muslim authors, all of which do honor to the prince whose history we have just written. Mildness, humanity, beneficence, piety, justice, liberality formed his particular character. We are told that his face inspired love more than respect; that his look did not have any of that pride which sometimes indicates masters of the world; that his speech was simple, polite, naturally eloquent; but that his imagination never rose to poetry, and rarely to those audacious figures, those metaphors so familiar to the Orient. He cultivated a kind of study that was very frivolous and much esteemed by the devout Muslims: that of being familiar with all the Muslim traditions, the explications of the Koran, the different sentiments of the interpreters, the different opinions of the schools; and he took pleasure in disputing on these matters with the priests and Cadhis. He little favored the poets and dialecticians then so common in the Orient, showered with favors the doctors of the law, and only persecuted writers who did not respect morality and religion in their works. He did not have any of those great passions that make men leave the ordinary sphere of life, passions that are so harmful to humanity when they agitate the soul of sovereigns. Greater by his tranquil and pacific virtues than by his martial exploits, nature seemed to have destined him to a private life rather than the government of a great state. He lacked that firmness which is so necessary to princes in order to have their power respected. He never established severe discipline among his troops, and restrained his Emirs more by his mildness, virtue and generosity than by the brake of his authority. Fortune placed him on a throne to which he had not aspired. The necessity of sustaining himself on it made him unpleasant to his benefactors. Religion more than politics placed arms in his hands and made him spill blood that he was loath to shed.

4

MOSES MENDELSSOHN

On Lessing

1786

Moses Mendelssohn (1729–1786) was regarded as the greatest Jewish philosopher of his century. He was a chief founder of the Haskalah *or Jewish Enlightenment, which sought to combine Enlightenment ideas and methods with Judaism. He was also one of the premier European philosophers of his day and a good friend of Lessing. The two men met in 1754 and maintained a warm and intellectually productive friendship until Lessing's death in 1781. Mendelssohn is widely regarded as the prototype of Nathan the Wise: a Jew who successfully synthesized rationality and religious faith. Four years after Lessing's death, and less than a year before his own, Mendelssohn reflected on the significance of Lessing's thought. In the passage below Mendelssohn reports a conversation with a friend, known simply as "D." To this day it is unclear who "D" was, but for our purposes that hardly matters, since this person's opinion of Lessing corresponds closely to Mendelssohn's own thinking. The excerpt begins with "D" speaking.*

"It is the greatest triumph of human wisdom to recognize the most perfect harmony between the system of intentions and the system of effective causes and to realize with Shaftesbury[1] and Leibniz[2] that

[1]Anthony Ashley Cooper, Third Earl of Shaftesbury (1671–1713), an English *philosophe.* [Ed.]
[2]For more on Leibniz, see the introduction to this volume and Document 5. [Ed.]

Excerpted from *Morgenstunden oder Vorlesungen über das Daseyn Gottes* [Morning hours or lectures on the presence of God] (Berlin, 1786), 265–71.

God's intentions, together with his assistance, apply to the smallest changes and to single occurrences in the existence of inanimate as well as animate creatures; that both the general laws of intentions and the general laws of effective causes emerge, in a perfectly harmonious way, out of the similarities among particular things, events and final goals; that there are never any gaps here, and that every natural effect corresponds as much to divine intentions as it flows from God's omnipotence. Recognizing God's reign and providence in the tiniest events, and recognizing these precisely because they are so tiny, since these things follow the usual course of nature; revering God more in natural events than in miracles; this, it seems to me, is the highest cultivation of human ideas, the most sublime way of thinking about God and his reign and providence."

I expressed my approval to him, and quoted the words of the rabbi who had already remarked on this matter of sublimity and good intentions: Wherever you find God's greatness and sublimity, you will also find his good intentions.[3] Most extraordinary are the passages from Scripture with which this teacher, according to the fashion of the rabbis, substantiates this teaching, and the lyrical energy that the Psalmist contributes:

> Who is like our God, the Eternal?
> Who is enthroned so high?
> Looks so deep?
> In Heaven?
> On Earth?[4]

D. continued: "Now it seems to me, friend, this teaching has never been expounded on by any writer with, on the one hand, more conviction and description of particular cases, and on the other hand, more ardor and pious inspiration, than by our immortal Lessing. Let us just recall those superb scenes in his dramatic didactic poem [*Nathan the Wise*], in which he has unmistakably portrayed, with all the clarity of the didactic philosopher and at the same time with all the energy of the theatrical poet, the true teaching of the providence and governance of God, as well as the harm in the kind of representation by which people always focus on the miraculous in order to recognize the finger of God. Such a combination was only possible with Lessing, and

---

[3]Mendelssohn is referring to Rabbi Yohanan in the Talmudic tractate *Megilla,* 31a. Cited in Alexander Altmann, *Moses Mendelssohn: A Biographical Study* (University: University of Alabama Press, 1973), 876n. [Ed.]

[4]Ps. 113:5–6. [Ed.]

perhaps only with him in our mother tongue. It appears that only our language has been able to achieve this kind of instruction, in which the language of reason is combined with the most lively depiction."

"It seems to me," I said, "as though Lessing had the intention with his *Nathan* to write a sort of *Anti-Candide*." The French poet [Voltaire] gathered all the forces of his wit, spurred the inexhaustible humor of his satirical mind, in a word, exerted all of the extraordinary talent that Providence had given him, in order to produce a satire against this very Providence. The German [Lessing] did precisely the same thing in order to justify Providence, to portray Him in the eyes of mortals in His purest state of blessedness. I can remember how my departed friend, soon after the appearance of *Candide,* had the fleeting idea of writing an appendix to it, or even more a sequel, in which he had the intention of showing through a series of events that all the evil which Voltaire heaped together and versified at the expense of a slandered Providence would nevertheless lead to the best and be found to be in harmony with His supremely wise intentions. It seemed that the French satirist had made the task too difficult for him, that he had piled up through poetry more evil than poetry could compensate for. Lessing preferred to take his own path, created a series of events that in terms of spirit and poetic power can be placed next to *Candide,* and which relates to the latter in the excellence of its intentions, in wisdom and usefulness, approximately as Heaven relates to Hell or as the ways of God relate to the ways of the Tempter."

"And precisely this great ode to Providence," D. continued, "precisely this blessed effort to justify the ways of God before human beings, how dearly our immortal friend paid for this! Oh! It embittered his final days, if it did not in the end actually cut his precious life short. Upon the publication of the *Fragmente*[5] he was already prepared to see himself attacked by the whole mob of writers, with or without qualification, who wanted to refute the *Fragmente,* and he considered himself strong enough to defend his guest[6] from all the unprovoked attacks of his opponents. So various were the ways in which his antagonists could strike, and when success appeared possible, how they truly struck, in their effort to fight him: yet he believed himself capable of defying all those who could not distinguish themselves through fairness and love of truth. In the end this remained, however vigorously he led the fight, just a schoolyard quarrel which led to some more or less unpleasant hours for the respective sides, but which he believed had not had any

<hr/>

[5]A controversial publication appearing in 1777. [Ed.]
[6]Reimarus, the unorthodox theologian whose views Lessing explicated in the *Fragmente.* [Ed.]

essential influence on the happiness of life. But how the scene changed
after the appearance of *Nathan*! Now the cabal thronged out of the
studies and bookshops and into the houses of his friends and acquaintances, and whispered in everyone's ear, 'Lessing has insulted *Christianity,* although he only dared to make a few accusations against a few
Christians and at most against *Christendom.*' In fact his *Nathan,* we
must admit, contributes to the true honor of Christendom. Upon what
high step of enlightenment and culture must a people stand, in which
a man can rise to this height of thinking and educate himself to such a
fine knowledge of divine and human matters! At least, it seems to me,
posterity will have to think so; but Lessing's contemporaries did not
think so. Every accusation of self-conceit and prejudice that [Lessing]
leveled, or had his dramatic characters level, against some of his coreligionists, each experienced as a personal insult from him. The completely welcome friend and acquaintance now found completely dry
faces, distant, frosty looks, cold receptions and cheerful partings, saw
himself abandoned by friends and acquaintances and left defenseless
against the snares of his persecutors. Strange! Among the most superstitious Frenchmen *Candide* did not have nearly such bad consequences for Voltaire, this libel against Providence did not draw nearly
as much animosity toward him as Lessing, through his *Nathan,* drew
from the most enlightened Germans for this defense of Providence,
and how sad were the effects of this on his mind!"

5

GOTTFRIED WILHELM LEIBNIZ

Theodicy

1710

*Gottfried Wilhelm Leibniz (1646–1716) is often considered the founder
of the* Aufklärung, *or German Enlightenment. A mathematician who
invented differential and integral calculus, Leibniz was also famous for*

Excerpted from Gottfried Wilhelm Leibniz, *Essais de Théodicée sur la bonté de Dieu, la
liberté de l'homme et l'origine du mal* [Essays of theodicy on the goodness of God, the
freedom of man and the origin of evil] (1710), reprinted in C. J. Gerhardt., ed., *Die
philosophischen Schriften von Gottfried Wilhelm Leibniz* (Berlin, 1885), 376–87.

his theodicy, or "justification of God." The main problem of theodicy was to show that God was both omnipotent (that is, all-powerful) and good despite the existence of evil in the world. Leibniz published his solution to this problem in Essais de Théodicée sur la bonté de Dieu, la liberté de l'homme et l'origine du mal *[Essays of theodicy on the goodness of God, the freedom of man and the origin of evil] (Amsterdam, 1710). A highly systematic thinker, Leibniz was able to reduce his many complex arguments throughout the book to a brief summary at the end. Although not a substitute for the book itself, this summary is a convenient introduction to Leibniz's religious philosophy. By extension, it helps to explain Lessing's own theodicy as elaborated in* Nathan the Wise.

SUMMARY OF THE CONTROVERSY REDUCED TO FORMAL ARGUMENTS

Certain intelligent persons have wished me to make this addition, and I deferred all the more readily to their advice in that I have thus had the chance to answer some objections and to make some observations that had not yet been sufficiently addressed in the work.

I. Objection

Whoever does not take the best course lacks power, or knowledge, or goodness.

God did not take the best course in creating this world.

Therefore God lacks power, or knowledge, or goodness.

RESPONSE

I deny the minor, that is to say the second premise of this syllogism,[1] and my adversary proves [me right] by this.

PROSYLLOGISM[2]

Whoever makes things in which there is evil, but which could be made without any evil, or whose production could have been omitted, does not take the best course.

---

[1]A syllogism is an argument that consists of three premises: a "major," a "minor," and a conclusion. [Ed.]

[2]A prosyllogism is a syllogism whose conclusion is the major or minor premise of a second syllogism. [Ed.]

God made a world in which there is evil; a world, I say, which could have been made without any evil, or whose production could have been completely omitted.

Therefore God did not take the right course.

RESPONSE

I grant the minor of this prosyllogism; for one must admit that there is evil in this world that God has made, and that it was possible to make a world without evil, or even not to create this world at all, since its creation depended upon God's free will. But I deny the major, that is to say the first of the two premises of the prosyllogism, and I could be content to ask for its proof; but to give additional clarification in this matter, I have wished to justify this negation by observing that the best course is not always the one that tends to avoid evil, since it could be that the evil is accompanied by a greater good. For example, an army general will prefer a great victory with a light injury to a situation without injury and without victory. I have shown that more completely in this work by showing through examples taken from mathematics, and elsewhere, that an imperfection in the part could be required for a greater perfection in the whole. In this I have followed the opinion of Saint Augustine,[3] who has said a hundred times that God permitted evil in order to draw good from it, that is to say a greater good; and [the opinion] of Thomas Aquinas,[4] who says . . . that permitting evil tends toward the good of the universe. I have shown that among the ancients the fall of Adam was called *felix culpa,* a happy sin, since amends were made for it, with an immense advantage, by the incarnation of the son of God, who gave the universe something more noble than anything it would have had without this one among its creatures. And for more clarification I have added with many good authors that it was for order and the general good that God left to certain creatures that opportunity to exercise their liberty, even when he predicted that they would turn to evil, but that God could so easily redress this, since it would not be appropriate, simply to prevent sin, for God always to act in an extraordinary way. It therefore suffices, to destroy the objection, to show that a world with evil could be better than a world without evil; but I have gone further still

---

　　[3]Saint Augustine of Hippo (354–430) was a Church Father and one of the most important Christian theologians ever. [Ed.]
　　[4]Saint Thomas Aquinas (1224/25–1274) was one of the chief Christian theologians of the Middle Ages. [Ed.]

in this work, and I have even shown that this universe must truly be better than any other possible universe.

II. Objection

If there is more evil than good in intelligent creatures, there is more evil than good in all of God's work.

But there is more evil than good in intelligent creatures.

Therefore there is more evil than good in all of God's work.

RESPONSE

I deny the major and the minor of this conditional syllogism. As to the major, I do not agree at all, because this supposed inference from the part to the whole, from intelligent creatures to all creatures, supposes tacitly and without proof that creatures deprived of reason cannot enter into comparison or share the same account with those who have it. But why could it not be that the surplus of good in the non-intelligent creatures that fill the world compensates for and even incomparably surpasses the surplus of evil in the reasonable creatures? It is true that the cost of the former is greater, but in recompense the others are incomparably more numerous; and it could be that the proportion of the number and the quantity surpasses that of the cost and the quality.

As to the minor, I must not admit it either, that is to say, I must not admit that there is more evil than good in intelligent creatures. I do not even have to agree that there is more evil than good in the human race, because it could be, and it is quite reasonable to believe, that the glory and the perfection of the blessed is incomparably greater than the misery and imperfection of the damned, and that here the excellence of the total good in the smaller number prevails over the total evil in the greater number. The blessed approach divinity by means of a divine mediator, insofar as it can be appropriate to these creatures, and make progress in good that it is impossible for the damned to make in evil even when they come as close as possible to the nature of demons. God is infinite, and the demon is limited; the good can go and does go toward infinity, whereas evil has its limits. It is therefore possible, and it is to be believed, that what happens in the comparison of the blessed and the damned is the opposite of what we have said can happen in the comparison of intelligent and non-intelligent creatures. That is to say, it could be that in the comparison of the happy and the miserable, the proportion of degrees surpasses that of numbers, and that in the comparison of intelligent and non-intelligent creatures, the proportion of numbers is greater than that of costs. One is right to suppose that a thing can be, as long as it cannot be proved impossible, and what I have advanced here even goes beyond supposition.

But in the second place, when one admits that there is more evil than good in the human race, one still has all reason not to admit that there is more evil than good in all intelligent creatures. For there is an inconceivable number of spirits, and there could be other reasonable creatures. And an adversary would not know how to prove that in all the City of God, composed as much of spirits as of innumerable reasonable animals from an infinity of species, evil surpasses good. And although one is not at all obligated when responding to an objection to prove that a thing is when its mere possibility suffices, I have not neglected to show in the present work that it is a consequence of the supreme perfection of the Sovereign of the universe that the Kingdom of God should be the most perfect of all possible states or governments, and that consequently the little evil that exists should be required for the full measure of the immense good that is found there.

III. Objection

If it is always impossible not to sin, it is always unjust to punish [sin].

Now it is always impossible not to sin, or rather every sin is necessary.

Therefore it is always unjust to punish [sin].

The minor is proved as follows.

1. PROSYLLOGISM

Everything that is predetermined is necessary.

Every event is predetermined.

Therefore every event (and consequently every sin as well) is necessary.

This second minor is again proved as follows.

2. PROSYLLOGISM

That which is in the future, that which is foreseen, that which is wrapped up in causes, is predetermined.

Every event is such.

Therefore every event is predetermined.

RESPONSE

I grant in a certain sense the conclusion of this second syllogism, which is the minor of the first; but I deny the major of the first syllogism, that is to say, that everything which is predetermined is necessary; understanding by the necessity of sinning, for example, or by the impossibility of not sinning, or of not doing some action, the necessity of which we are speaking here, that is to say that [necessity] which is essential and absolute, and which destroys the morality of action and the justice of punishments. For if one meant a different necessity or impossibility (that is to say a necessity which was only moral, or only hypothetical, which will be explained presently), it is obvious that we would deny the major of the objection itself. One might be content with this response and ask proof for the denied proposition; but I am happy to justify the procedure I have used in the present work to clarify the matter better and to shed more light on it by explaining the necessity that must be rejected and the determination that must take place. Necessity contrary to morality, which must be avoided and which would make punishment unjust, is an insurmountable necessity, which would make all opposition pointless, even if one wanted with all one's heart to avoid the necessary action and made all possible efforts toward this end. Now it is obvious that this is not applicable to voluntary actions, since one would not do them if one did not want to. Their foreseeability and predetermination is therefore not absolute, but presuppose will: if it is certain that one will do them, it is no less sure that one will want to do them. These voluntary actions, and their consequences, will not happen, whatever one does, whether one likes it or not; but because one will do, and will want to do, what leads to them. And this is contained in foreseeability and predetermination, and in fact even in reason. And the necessity of certain events is called conditional or hypothetical, or rather necessity of consequence, because it presupposes will and the other prerequisites; as opposed to the necessity that destroys morality and makes punishment unjust and recompense pointless, which is in the things that will be, whatever one does or wants to do since it is, in a word, in that which is essential: and this is what one calls an absolute necessity. There is therefore no point, with respect to what is absolutely necessary, to make prohibitions or commandments, to suggest penalties or rewards, to blame or praise: it will happen just the same. Yet in voluntary actions and what depends on them, precepts, armed with the power to punish and reward, very often work, and are included in the order of causes that make action exist. And it is for this reason that not only effort and work, but also prayers, are useful, since God has already taken these prayers into account before settling matters and has had proper regard for them. This is why the precept that says *ora et labora* (pray and work) survives intact; and not only those who claim (under the vain pretext of the necessity of events) that one can neglect the efforts that things call for, but also those who reason against prayer, fall into what the ancients already called the lazy sophism.[5] Thus the predetermination of events by causes is precisely what contributes to morality, instead of destroying it, and causes give inclinations to the will without necessitating it. This is why the determination in question is not at all a necessitation: it is certain (to him who knows all) that the effect will follow this inclination; but this effect does not follow from it by a necessary consequence, that is to say, whose opposite implies a contradiction: and it is also by such an internal inclination that the will is determined, without there being necessity. Suppose that one had the greatest passion in the world (for example, a great thirst), you will admit to me that the soul could find some reason to resist it, even if this were only to show its power. Thus although one may never be in a state of perfect indifference of balance, and may always have a prevalence of inclination for the action that one takes, this prevalence never makes the resolution that one takes absolutely necessary.

IV. Objection

Whoever can prevent the sin of another and does not do so, but even contributes to it, although he is well informed of it, is complicit in it.

God can prevent the sin of intelligent creatures; but he does not, and he even contributes to it by his cooperation and by the opportunities he brings into existence, although he has perfect knowledge of this.

Therefore [God is complicit in human sin].

RESPONSE

I deny the major of this syllogism. For it is possible that one could prevent sin but that one ought not to do so, because one could not do so

---

[5]A sophism is a false argument designed only to show the cleverness of the person who makes it. The term derives from the Sophists, professional teachers of philosophy in ancient Athens who reputedly cared more about winning arguments than arriving at the truth. [Ed.]

without committing a sin oneself or (in God's case) without perform-
ing an unreasonable action. I have given examples of this, even where
God himself is concerned. It is also possible that one could contribute
to evil and even sometimes open the way to it by doing the things that
one is obligated to do. And when one does one's duty or (in God's
case) when, having considered everything thoroughly, one does what
reason asks, one is not responsible for the events, not even when one
foresees them. One does not want these evils; but one wants to permit
them for a greater good that one cannot reasonably excuse oneself
from preferring to other considerations. And this is a *consequent* will
that results from *antecedent* wills by which one wants the good. I know
that some people, when speaking of the antecedent and consequent
will of God, have meant by the *antecedent* will that which wants all
men to be saved, and by the *consequent* that which wants, as a result
of persistent sin, that some people be damned, since damnation is a
consequence of sin. But these are only some examples of a more general notion, and one could say with as much reason that God wants
with his antecedent will that men not sin, and that with his consequent
or final and decreeing will (which always has its effect) he wants to
permit them to sin, since this permission is a consequence of superior
reasons. And one has reason to say in general that God's antecedent
will works toward the production of good and the prevention of evil,
each taken in itself, and as though detached . . . according to the measure of the degree of each good or each evil; but that the consequent,
final and total divine will works toward the production of as many
good things as can be put together, whose combination becomes in
that way determined, and also includes the permission for some evil
things and the exclusion of some good things, as the best possible
plan for the universe requires. . . .

V. Objection

Whoever produces all that is real in a thing is its cause.

God produces all that is real in sin.

Therefore God is the cause of sin.

RESPONSE

I could be content to deny the major or the minor, since the term
"real" allows interpretations that could render these propositions false.
But in order to explain myself better I shall distinguish [between two

things]. "Real" either means that which is only positive or also includes privative beings: in the first case, I deny the major and grant the minor; in the second case, the reverse. I could limit myself to this; but I have rather wished to go further still in order to justify this distinction. I have therefore been very happy to consider that every purely positive or absolute reality is a perfection, and that every imperfection comes from limitation, that is to say, from the privative: for to limit is to refuse progress or the most. Now God is the cause of all perfections, and consequently of all realities, when one considers them as purely positive. But the limitations, or the privations, result from the original imperfection of creatures which limits their receptivity. And it is as in the case of a full boat that the river moves more or less slowly in proportion to the weight it carries: thus the speed comes from the river, but the slowing that limits this speed comes from the cargo. I have also shown in the present work how the creature, by causing sin, is a deficient cause; how errors and bad inclinations are born of privation; and how privation is effective by accident. And I have justified the opinion of Saint Augustine . . . who explains (for example) how God hardens people, not by giving something bad to the soul, but because the effect of its good impression is limited by the soul's resistance and by the circumstances that contribute to this resistance, such that he does not give it all the good that might overcome its evil. *Nec (inquit) ab illo erogatur aliquid quo homo fit deterior, sed tantum quo fit melior non erogatur.*[6] But if God had wanted to do more here, he would have had to make either other kinds of creatures or other miracles, in order to change their natures, which the best plan could not have allowed. It is as if it were necessary that the river's current be faster than its slope permitted, or that the boats be less full, in order for these boats to be pushed with greater speed. And the original limitation or imperfection of creatures requires that even the best plan for the universe would not allow more good things and not be exempted from certain evil things, which nevertheless must lead to a greater good. There are some disorders in the parts which marvelously increase the beauty of the whole, just as some dissonances, properly used, make the harmony more beautiful. But that depends on what I have already said in response to the first objection.

---

[6]"The man," he [Aquinas] says, "is not given by him something that he makes worse, but such as he does not make better." [Ed.]

VI. Objection

Whoever punishes those who have done as well as it is in their power to do is unjust.

God does it.

Therefore [God is unjust].

RESPONSE

I deny the minor of this argument. And I believe that God always gives sufficient aid and grace to those who have good will, that is to say, who do not reject this grace with a new sin. Thus I do not agree that children who have died without baptism or outside the Church are damned, nor do I believe in the damnation of adults who have acted according to the enlightenment that God gave them. And I believe that if *anyone has followed the enlightenment that he has,* he will indubitably receive more of it than he needs, as the late Mr. Hulseman, the famous and profound theologian of Leipzig, has remarked somewhere; and if such a man had been missing enlightenment during his life, he would at least receive it at the moment of his death.

VII. Objection

Whoever gives only to some, and not to all, the means of obtaining good will and the final saving faith, does not have enough goodness.

God does it.

Therefore [God does not have enough goodness].

RESPONSE

I deny the major. It is true that God could overcome the greatest resistance of the human heart, and he sometimes does it too, either by internal grace or by external circumstances that can do much to souls: but he does not always do it. "Where does this distinction come from," one will say, "and why does [God's] goodness appear to be limited?" It is that it would not have been in accordance with order for [God] always to act extraordinarily, and to reverse the connection of things, as I have already remarked in the first objection. The reasons for this connection, according to which one is placed in more favorable circumstances than another, are hidden in the depth of God's wisdom: they depend upon the universal harmony. The best plan for the universe, which God could not fail to choose, produced this connection.

One judges it according to the event itself; since God made it, it was not possible to make it better. Far from this conduct being in opposition to goodness, it is supreme goodness which has made it thus. This objection together with its solution could have been inferred from what has been said regarding the first objection; but it seemed useful to treat it separately.

VIII. Objection

Whoever cannot fail to choose the best is not free.

God cannot fail to choose the best.

Therefore God is not free.

RESPONSE

I deny the major of this argument. It is rather true liberty, and the most perfect [liberty], to be able to make the best of one's free will, and to exercise this power always, without being diverted either by external force or internal passion, one of which enslaves the body and the other of which enslaves the soul. There is nothing less servile and more appropriate to the highest degree of liberty than to be always directed toward the good, and always by one's own inclination, without any constraint, and without any displeasure. And to object that God therefore needed external things is nothing but a sophism. He creates them freely: but having proposed an end, which is to exercise his goodness, [his] wisdom determined him to choose the most proper means of achieving that end. To call that *need* is to take the term in an extraordinary sense, which purges it of all imperfection, much as one does when speaking of God's anger.

Seneca[7] says somewhere that God only commanded one time, but that he obeys always, because he obeys the laws that he wanted to prescribe for himself; *semel jussit, semper paret*.[8] But he could better have said that God commands always and that he is always obeyed. For by willing he always follows the leaning of his own nature, and all other things always follow his will. And as this will is always the same, one cannot say that he only obeys the will he had previously. Nevertheless, although his will is always infallible and always tends toward

---

[7]Seneca (4 B.C.E.–65 C.E.) was a Roman Stoic philosopher who believed in predestination. [Ed.]

[8]"He ordered once, he obeys always." [Ed.]

the best, evil or the lesser good that he rejects does not cease to be possible in itself; otherwise the necessity of the good would be geometrical (so to speak) or metaphysical, and completely absolute. The contingency of things would be destroyed and there would be no choice. But this type of necessity, which does not destroy the possibility of the opposite, only has this name by analogy; it becomes effective not by the sole essence of things, but by that which is outside of them and above them, that is to say by the will of God. This necessity is called moral [necessity] because, for the wise person, "necessary" and "due" are equivalent things. And if it always has its effect, as it truly has in the perfect sage, that is to say in God, one may say that this is a happy necessity. The closer creatures come to it, the closer they come to perfect felicity. Also this type of necessity is not the kind one tries to avoid and which destroys morality, rewards, praise. For what it brings does not arrive whatever one does, but because one has willed it. And a will for which it is natural to choose well is the most praiseworthy. Also it brings its own reward with it, which is sovereign happiness. And as this constitution of the Divine Nature gives complete satisfaction to whoever possesses it, it is also the best and the most desirable for the creatures that all depend upon God. If the will of God did not have as its rule the principle of the best, it would tend to evil, which would be the worst; or rather it would be completely indifferent to good or evil and would be guided by chance. But a will that always lets itself be guided by chance would not be any better at governing the universe than the haphazard cooperation of corpuscles without there being any Divinity. And even if God only abandoned himself to chance in certain cases and in certain ways (as he would if he did not always tend entirely toward the best, and if he were capable of preferring a lesser good to a greater good, that is to say an evil to a good, since that which prevents a greater good is an evil) he would be imperfect, just as imperfect as the object of his choice. He would not deserve our complete trust; he would act without reason in such a case and the government of the universe would be like certain games divided equally between reason and chance. And all this shows that this objection that one makes to the choice of the best perverts the notions of the free and the necessary, and represents the best to us as a bad thing: which is either malicious or ridiculous.

A Gotthold Ephraim Lessing Chronology (1729–1786)

1729 Birth of Gotthold Ephraim Lessing in Kamenz (Saxony).

Birth of Moses Mendelssohn in Dessau (Anhalt-Dessau).

1746–1748 Lessing's university years in Leipzig (Saxony).

1749 Publication of Lessing's *Die Juden* [The Jews], a one-act play decrying anti-Jewish prejudice.

1751–1752 Lessing earns a Master's degree in medicine at the University of Wittenberg (Saxony).

1754 Lessing and Mendelssohn meet in Berlin.

1767 Lessing works as director and critic at the "German National Theater" in Hamburg.

Publication and stage production of Lessing's *Minna von Barnhelm*.

1770 Lessing becomes chief librarian at the Ducal Library of Wolfenbüttel.

1776 Lessing's marriage to Eva König.

1777 Birth and death of Lessing's son Traugott (December 25).

1778 Death of Eva König (January 10).

1779 Publication of *Nathan the Wise*.

1781 Lessing's death.

1783 First public performance of *Nathan the Wise*.

1786 Mendelssohn's death.

Questions for Consideration

1. What are the qualities that make Nathan "wise"? Which specific actions or attitudes qualify him for this title?

2. The word *Mensch* ("human being") occurs frequently in *Nathan the Wise.* What does it mean to Lessing?

3. What is the meaning of the Parable of the Rings (3, 7)? Is it a satisfactory answer to Saladin's question to Nathan (3, 5)? How does Saladin respond to the parable, and what does this say about his character?

4. In Act 1, Scene 3 Nathan says, "No one has to have to," suggesting a belief in human freedom. Yet in Act 5, Scene 4 he addresses God as one who does not "have to judge human beings by their deeds, which so rarely are their deeds," and elsewhere suggests that God has pre-ordained all of human history. Does Nathan believe in free will or not? What is Lessing's view on the matter?

5. Some readers of Lessing have seen him as an early feminist. On the basis of your reading of *Nathan the Wise,* is this claim accurate?

6. How has Nathan educated his daughter Recha? What might his method say about Lessing's attitude toward the education of women in particular or toward education in general?

7. Although *Nathan the Wise* is primarily about high ideals, it also concerns money. What role does money play? How do the various characters relate to it, and how do their attitudes in this regard define them?

8. What do you think of the Templar? Is he a sympathetic or an unsympathetic character? Does he develop as a character during the course of the play? If so, how?

9. Some critics have charged that *Nathan the Wise,* while affirming the equality of Judaism, Christianity, and Islam, is not entirely free of prejudice. Is this claim justified?

10. What does it mean to be Jewish in *Nathan the Wise*? What, if anything, makes Nathan Jewish? What, if anything, makes Recha Jewish?

11. Most of the Christian characters in *Nathan the Wise* have significant moral failings. Does this mean that Lessing was critical of Christianity? If not, then why did he portray Christians as he did?

Selected Bibliography

Most of the books and articles about Lessing are, not surprisingly, in German. Nevertheless, there are several insightful and thought-provoking works on Lessing in English. The following is a selected list of these studies. For a more complete and systematic bibliography, including works in German as well as English, see Doris Kuhles and Erdmann von Wilamowitz-Moellendorff, *Lessing-Bibliographie 1971–1985* (Berlin: Aufbau, 1988).

BOOKS

Allison, Henry E. *Lessing and the Enlightenment: His Philosophy of Religion and its Relation to Eighteenth-Century Thought*. Ann Arbor: University of Michigan Press, 1966.
Eckardt, Jo-Jacqueline. *Lessing's Nathan the Wise and the Critics, 1779–1991*. Columbia, S.C.: Camden House, 1993.
Garland, Henry B. *Lessing: The Founder of Modern German Literature*. London and New York: Macmillan & Co. and St. Martin's Press, 1962.
Lamport, F[rancis]. J[ohn]. *Lessing and the Drama*. Oxford: Clarendon Press, 1981.
Yasukata, Toshimasa. *Lessing's Philosophy of Religion and the German Enlightenment: Lessing on Christianity and Reason*. Oxford: Oxford University Press, 2002.

ARTICLES

Angress, Ruth K. "'Dreams That Were More Than Dreams' in Lessing's *Nathan*." In *Lessing Yearbook* 3 (1971): 108–27.
Atkins, Stuart. "The Parable of the Rings in Lessing's 'Nathan der Weise.'" In *The Germanic Review* 26 (Spring 1951): 259–67.
Bennett, Benjamin. "Reason, Error and the Shape of History: Lessing's Nathan and Lessing's God." In *Lessing Yearbook* 9 (1977): 60–80.
Bohnert, Christiane. "Enlightenment and Despotism: Two Worlds in Lessing's *Nathan the Wise*." In *Impure Reason: Dialectic of Enlightenment in Germany*. Edited by W. Daniel Wilson and Robert C. Holub. Detroit: Wayne State University Press, 1993. 344–63.

Goetschel, Willi. "Negotiating Truth: On Nathan's Business." In *Lessing Yearbook* 28 (1996): 105–24.

John, David. "Lessing, Islam and *Nathan the Wise* in Africa." In *Lessing Yearbook* 32 (2000): 245–60.

Kaynar, Gad. "Lessing and Non-Lessing on the Israeli Stage: Notes on Some Theological, Political and Theatrical Aspects." In *Lessing Yearbook* 32 (2000): 361–70.

Kowalik, Jill Anne. "*Nathan* as a Work of Mourning." In *Lessing Yearbook* 21 (1989): 1–18.

Leventhal, Robert S. "The Parable as Performance: Interpretation, Cultural Transmission and Political Strategy in Lessing's 'Nathan der Weise.'" In *German Quarterly* 61 (Fall 1988): 502–28.

Oesmann, Astrid. "*Nathan der Weise:* Suffering Lessing's 'Erzeihung.'" In *The Germanic Review* 74 (Spring 1999) 131–45.

Whiton, John. "Aspects of Reason and Emotion in Lessing's *Nathan der Weise*." In *Lessing Yearbook* 9 (1977): 45–59.

Index

Faustus Society, 133*n*
felix culpa (happy sin), 155
feminism, 3
Fragmente (Lessing), 152
Frederick I ("Barbarossa"), 43
Frederick the Great, 2, 5
French Revolution, 7
Frothingham, Ellen, 17–18

Galen, 38*n*
Ganges River, 35
Gath, 97
German Enlightenment (*Aufklärung*),
vii–ix, 153
German National Theater, 165
God
antecedent and consequent will of, 160
as cause of sin, 160–61
evil and, 153, 155
evil in work of, 156–57
freedom to choose by, 163–64
goodness of, 154–56, 162–63
Leibniz's justification for, 153–64
predetermination of, 157–59
prevention of sin and, 159–60
religious diversity and, 15–16
Goethe, 17
Guebres, 61

Haskalah (Jewish Enlightenment), 150
Hegira, 145
History of Saladin (Marin), 14, 139–50
Hofmann, Sigismund, 125
Holocaust, 18, 20
Holy Sepulchre, 87
honor, 2–3
Hospitaler brothers, 141
humility, 15–16

iambic pentameter, xi–xii
iambs, xi
idolatry, 44
Iffland, August Wilhelm, 25*f*
Imam, 44
Index Librorum Prohibitorum, 17
Islam, 130*n. See also* Muslims
prejudice toward, 4, 139–40
Israel, 18

Jamerlonk, 88
Jerusalem, 10
Jesus, 87*n*, 95*n*
Jewish Enlightenment (Haskalah), 150
"Jewry Revealed" (Eisenmenger), 121–27
Jews
agriculture rights, 137–38
anti-Semitism, 18, 121–27
as Chosen People, 19, 56–57
commerce and moneylending by, 4–5,
34*n*, 129–30, 137
discrimination against, 4–7, 128–39

education of, 138
in eighteenth-century Europe, 4–10
emancipation of, 7
employment of, 129, 137
enlightenment of, 133–39
expelled from Austria, 123
grounds for denying rights to, 130
hatred of, by Christians, 135–36, 138–39
Jewish characters in *Nathan the Wise,* 4
living conditions, 134–36
moral corruptness of, 134–36
moral education of, 138
potential of, 8
prejudice toward, 4, 8, 138–39
reactions to discrimination, 131–32
religious freedom of, 136–37
removing discriminatory laws against,
128–39
rights of, 136–39
as ritual murderers, 121–27
settlement restrictions, 128–29
taxation of, 4, 7, 129, 137
Jews, The (*Die Juden*) (Lessing), 8, 16–17,
165
John I, king of England, 46*n*

Kant, Immanuel, 7
König, Eva, 165

Leibniz, Gottfried Wilhelm, ix, 7, 15, 20,
150, 163*n*
"Theodicy," 153–64
Lent, Johannes à, 124
Leopold I of Austria, 123
Lessing, G. E. (Gotthold Ephraim)
birth of, 165
career, 1–2
chronology, 165
death of, 17, 165
family, 1
marriage, 2, 165
Mendelssohn and, 7–10
Mendelssohn's views on, 150–53
plays, 2–3
portrait, 3*f*
publications, 2–3, 165
relevance of, 17–18
respect for religions by, 14–16
response to *Nathan the Wise* and, 16–17
writing style, xi–xiii
Luther, Martin, 132–33*n*
Lutheran church, 2

Madame the Patriarchess, 141
Mamelukes, 100
Mammon, 52
Marin, François-Louis-Claude, ix, 14
"History of Saladin," 139–50
Maronites, 41
Mary, mother of Emperor Manuel Com-
nenus, 140*n*